THE
HEBRIDEAN
BAKER

My Scottish Island Kitchen

THE
HEBRIDEAN BAKER

My Scottish Island Kitchen

COINNEACH MACLEOD

PHOTOGRAPHY BY SUSIE LOWE

BLACK & WHITE PUBLISHING

First published in the UK in 2022 by
Black & White Publishing Ltd
Nautical House, 104 Commercial Street, Edinburgh, EH6 6NF

A division of Bonnier Books UK
4th Floor, Victoria House, Bloomsbury Square, London, WC1B 4DA
Owned by Bonnier Books
Sveavägen 56, Stockholm, Sweden

All photography by Susie Lowe
Cover design by Henry Steadman

A CIP catalogue record for this book is available from the British Library.

ISBN: 978 1 78530 410 1

1 3 5 7 9 10 8 6 4 2

Design by Black & White
Printed and bound in Great Britain by Bell & Bain Ltd, Glasgow

www.blackandwhitepublishing.com

A Phàdruig

I'm so lucky to have you with me on this amazing adventure. Thank you for inspiring me every day and for being the best Hebridean Baker cake tester in the world!

Tha gaol agam ort, Coinneach x

CONTENTS

1
SCOTTISH RECIPES

2
CAKES & BISCUITS

3
COSY
WEEKEND DISHES

4
BREAD & SCONES

5
AFTERNOON TEA RECIPES

6
NORDIC BAKES

7
PIES & PUDS

8
NOLLAIG CHRIDHEIL

FÀILTE

What is my perfect island day?

Climbing over the Cromore hills to get the best view of the island, running into the ocean at Horgabost and running straight back out when my toes start to tingle with the cold, walking to the lighthouse in Scalpay to watch the boats sail by and stopping at my aunty's for a cuppa before heading home and getting ready to bake.

Fàilte, I'm Coinneach the Hebridean Baker and welcome to my Scottish island kitchen.

If this is the first time you have bought one of my books, thank you – I hope you absolutely love it. If this is your second Hebridean Baker book, welcome back, it's great to see you again! In this cookbook, I want to share recipes filled with the tradition, Scottish flavours and local ingredients that you will love to use in your kitchen. These simple, easy to make dishes invite you to gather friends and family around your table. It takes more than a peat fire and woolly socks to get through a Hebridean winter, so in this book you're going to find warming casseroles, hearty soups, perfect biscuits to dunk in your tea, comforting desserts and a cocktail or two that'll definitely put hairs on your chest!

I want to tell the stories behind the recipes and for you to meet the folk who love baking them. Some recipes I've found in my old cookbooks, sometimes I've persuaded friends and family to share their favourites and there are lots of new recipes too, but all have the seal of approval from the 'Official Hebridean Baker Cake Taster' – Pàdruig!

The landscapes, history and culture of the Outer Hebrides of Scotland are what make our islands unique. There is a word in Gaelic – *cianalas*. It describes the feeling of longing for somewhere, of a sense of place. That the Hebrides will be with you, wherever you are in the world. No matter how long you've been away, no matter where you live, you know the islands are your home. That anticipation as you stand on the deck of the CalMac ferry crossing the Minch, the views over the snow-topped hills as you drive over the Clisham, that perfect summer's day on Mangersta beach when you think the blue skies will last forever or the wild autumn storms when you realise they won't. The saying *Bi cianalas air Leòdhasach ann an nèamh* means a Lewisman would be homesick in heaven. Amen to that.

So as I turn off the stove on another book of my favourite recipes, I want to say thank you to my fellow islanders and friends around the world who have supported this wonderful adventure. It's because of you that I am back in my kitchen again and I have loved every minute of creating these recipes and stories. So, let's get baking!

HINTS & TIPS

Throughout *The Hebridean Baker*, I use certain preparation and baking techniques that I have learned work for me, but you might have your own way that works just as well. I'd love you to put a twist on my recipes!

When I list the following basics for a recipe, unless stated otherwise, I'd like you to use:

- **Butter.** Unsalted.
- **Eggs.** Medium.
- **Milk.** Whole.
- **Oats.** Rolled.
- **Sugar.** Caster.

Most of my ingredients should be readily available. If they aren't, normally there is an easy replacement. For example, you can substitute:

- **Black treacle** with molasses.
- **Bicarbonate of soda** with baking soda.
- **Double cream** with whipping cream.
- **Mixed spice** with pumpkin spice mix.

But, I have to be honest, golden syrup is quite unique. If it isn't the core ingredient of the recipe, corn syrup will work, but my recommendation? Hunt for it far and wide, you won't regret it!

Finally, can I recommend that you purchase digital kitchen scales – they are life changing! And while you are in your local kitchen shop, pick up a 1lb loaf tin (450g); I use this size for all my small bakes.

I find that a fan oven is the most reliable to achieve a perfect bake, but if you have a different type of oven, here is a handy conversion chart:

°C Fan	°C	°F	Gas Mark
130	150	300	2
140	160	325	3
150	170	340	
160	180	350	4
170	190	375	5
180	200	400	6
190	210	410	
200	220	425	
210	230	450	7
220	240	465	

COINNEACH'S LARDER

I am passionate about using home-grown Hebridean and Scottish produce. Eating locally first means choosing food that is grown and harvested close to where you live, investing in the local community and its people. Here are some of my favourite producers of quality foods that I use in my kitchen. I'd love you to give them a try!

CHARLES MACLEOD BUTCHER
CHARLESMACLEOD.CO.UK

For the finest Stornoway Black Pudding and the warmest welcome on the island, visit the iconic Charlie Barley's shop in Stornoway on the Isle of Lewis. Made to the original seventy-year-old recipe, their black puddings are legendary.

EAT DRINK HEBRIDES TRAIL
VISITOUTERHEBRIDES.CO.UK/FOOD-DRINK

The Outer Hebrides have some of the very best seafood, smokehouses, distilleries and crofting produce. Artisan producers showcase the best that our Atlantic larder has to offer. With an abundance of fresh local produce, you can follow the Eat Drink Hebrides Trail, which is a self-guided journey through the islands.

ISLE OF HARRIS DISTILLERY
HARRISDISTILLERY.COM

The distillery opened in 2015 in the village of Tarbert, on the Isle of Harris. You will be greeted at the distillery by a cosy peat fire and the friendly team. You can take guided tours, visit the shop and pick up some homemade bakes at the café. Flavoured with local, hand-harvested sugar kelp, Harris Gin comes in a beautifully distinctive bottle.

JURA WHISKY
JURAWHISKY.COM

The wee island of Jura distils my favourite dram; treat yourself to a bottle of their eighteen-year-old whisky for a special occasion. While you are on Lewis, stop by the Island Spirit Whisky Shop in Stornoway, specialising in quality, rare and exclusive Scotch Whisky, premium Scottish Gin and other artisan craft spirits.

STAG BAKERIES
STAGBAKERIES.CO.UK

A Hebridean institution since 1885, this artisan bakery in Stornoway uses traditional methods and only the finest ingredients. Add a healthy measure of creativity and you have a range of award-winning products for every occasion – water biscuits, oatcakes and shortbread.

BANAIS

Ma tha thu airson do mholadh, bàsaich;
ma tha thu airson do chàineadh, pòs!

If you want to be praised, die; if you want
to be criticised, marry!

I always come home from a wedding with
a story or two, be it spinning round the
dancefloor to a Strip the Willow with my
cousin Margaret, the time Aunt Bellag made
the best duff ever for my brother Dòmhnall's
wedding cake or, like many folk, promising
never to drink whisky again after a night of
too many drams – maybe a story too familiar
to us all!

Dòmhnall got married to his Welsh wife,
Zoe, on the banks of Loch Caitiosbhal in
Marvig on the Isle of Lewis. As family and
friends got ready for the big day, my brother
headed out on his boat to catch the wedding
dinner. Lobsters, crabs and fresh fish were
prepared as we fitted into our MacLeod
tartan kilts. After the vows, we walked back
to the village hand in hand and the duff was
sliced for all the guests. Songs and dancing
filled the house. It felt like a wedding I imagine
my Granny Anna Sheonaidh would have had
when she married Dòmhnall Sheumais nearly
a hundred years ago.

Our island weddings have been filled
with traditions and stories for centuries

and, in days gone by, the celebrations would
begin weeks ahead of the day itself with the
rèiteach. The villagers would be invited to the
house of the bride, where her father would sit
sternly awaiting his future son-in-law. When
he arrived, he would not be welcomed by his
bride, but by a series of old ladies from the
village who would, for fun, try and persuade
him to marry them instead! After politely
declining each one's advances, his bride would
finally appear. The mother of the bride would
then hand them a ball of yarn that was full
of knots. If they were able to untangle it, it
foretold that they would be able to solve any
challenges they had during their marriage. It
was then time for the groom to ask her father
for his daughter's hand in marriage. He would
often remind them of the Gaelic saying *Tha
am pòsadh coltach ri seillean – tha mil ann
's tha gath ann!* 'Marriage is like a bee, it has
the honey and the sting!' Once he agreed, the
bride and groom would drink whisky from
a quaich in front of the whole community,
beginning a night of cèilidh dancing and
drinking that lasted until the wee hours of
the morning.

It was only after the *rèiteach* that the real
wedding planning could begin. Though the
rèiteach was seen as a night of village fun,
it was an important event, sometimes as
important as the wedding day itself, as it was

considered a solemn and binding contract by the bride and groom and their families which could not be broken.

According to island traditions it is unlucky to marry in the month of May. Though there are many tales of why, it might have been because of the ill-fated Mary, Queen of Scots' marriage to the Earl of Bothwell in May 1567, which led to a series of events that would end with her beheading.

Mary was already a widow at eighteen when her husband, King Francis II of France, died. In February 1567, there was an explosion at the Edinburgh house of her second husband, Lord Darnley. However, that is not what killed him: his body lay outside of the property, unharmed in the explosion. He had been strangled. Suspicion for Darnley's murder fell on the Earl of Bothwell, Mary's third husband.

Mary was confronted at the Battle of Carberry Hill and imprisoned at Loch Leven Castle. However, she escaped and managed to gather an army in an attempt to take Scotland back. They were defeated at the Battle of Langside and Mary fled across the border to England. She hoped her cousin, Queen Elizabeth I, would help her get her throne back. Instead she was arrested for treason and eventually executed, as suspicions rose that Mary was plotting to take the throne of England.

Don't let this put you off getting married in the Hebrides in May too much, as it is usually during this month that we get to enjoy some of our finest weather. Just don't go planning to overthrow the monarchy any time soon after the wedding!

Preparations for the big day were a village occasion and all the women would visit the wedding house, *taigh na bainnse,* to help with the arrangements. Each family would gift a flock of chickens and a day was set aside for the village ladies to come and pluck them. Songs and laughter would be heard from the croft all that day with the women in a festive mood. I like to think of this as the Hebridean version of a 'hen night'! Once the chickens were prepared, they would all arrive at the post office, where parcels would have been delivered from family and friends on the mainland, who would have been tasked with finding the latest fashions in the fancy department stores of Glasgow and Edinburgh to be worn on the day. Even if it didn't rival Paris Fashion Week, there definitely was an air of Harris Fashion Week in the post office that day!

The eve of the wedding day, the bride and groom would be in their family homes to greet the arrival of their closest friends. To bless the marriage with good luck and fortune, it was tradition that they would have their shoes and socks removed and their feet washed while songs were sung and drams were drunk.

Over moorland and heather, lochs and seas, the guests would arrive on the day of the wedding to see white flags fluttering from homemade flagpoles outside each house. Bedsheets, tablecloths, pillowcases and a few pairs of large knickers would be flown and the arrival of the newlyweds was greeted with a gun salute by each of the men in the village. The bride would place a sixpence in her shoe for the walk to the church to bring her good fortune on her special day.

The piper would lead the procession back from the church after the wedding. As they passed the bride's house, her mother would meet her carrying a traditional round of shortbread, which she would break over the bride's head for luck. The guests would rush to collect a piece of the broken shortbread, as it possessed the ability to foretell the future if put under your pillow that night. It was often

said that whoever you dreamed of that night would be your future husband or wife.

The father of the bride would host the dinner in his barn. Most often there were more guests than chairs, so the people were taken to the wedding table in relays to toast the health of the bride and groom.

No island wedding would be complete without a cèilidh. The musicians would play strathspeys, reels and schottisches, and the dancing would go on till late in the night. And the wedding celebrations would not end there: the following night the bride and groom would host a *banais-taighe* – a house wedding. This would be a more low-key affair for the elderly folk in the village to spend time with the newlyweds.

All those weeks of celebrations finally at an end, folk would begin planning the next village wedding, every time with this wee Gaelic poem being read:

Saoghal fada, sona dhut,
Do cholunn fallain, slàn
Do bhoth gun bhoinne snighe ann,
Do chiste-mine làn

'May you have a long happy life,
A sound and healthy body,
A cottage that does not leak
And a larder that is always full'

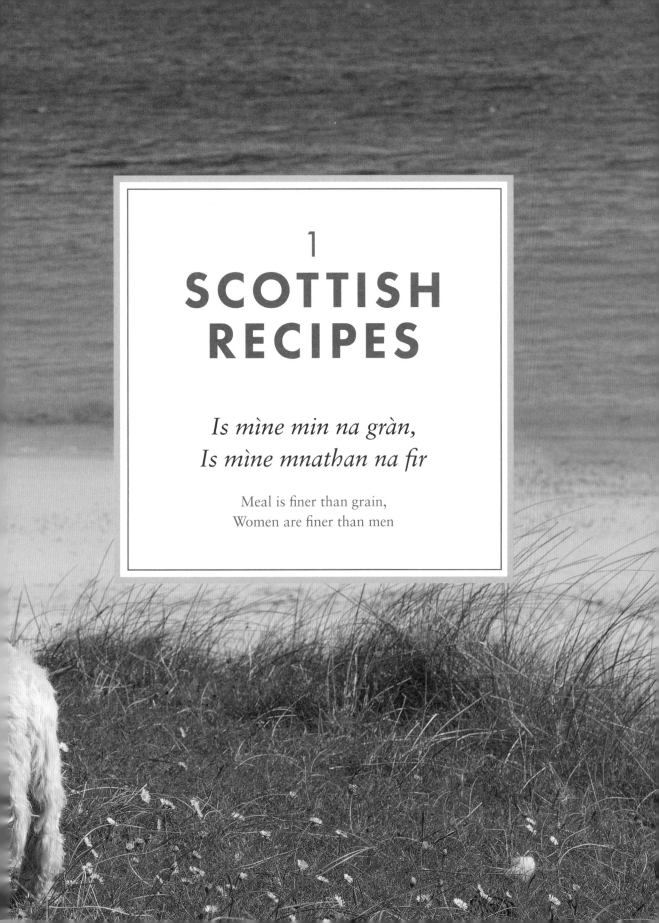

1
SCOTTISH RECIPES

Is mìne min na gràn,
Is mìne mnathan na fir

Meal is finer than grain,
Women are finer than men

WHISKY MARMALADE

MAKES **4** JARS

INGREDIENTS

6 oranges

1 lemon

1 litre (1 quart) water

1.1kg (2lb 7oz) preserving
sugar

2 tablespoons whisky

This might be the perfect marriage of Scottish flavours – and it's a wedding I would definitely go to! The sharp bitterness of the oranges is complimented with the warmth of the whisky. The lengthy cooking time ensures that the orange flavour is retained and some of the bitterness is tempered while the peel becomes beautifully soft. The splash of whisky at the end is quite subtle but well worth it!

METHOD

Slice the oranges in quarters, scoop out the flesh and blend until smooth in a food processor. Push the purée through a muslin into a saucepan. What's left in the muslin cloth can be discarded.

Take the quarters of orange peel and slice the rind into matchsticks. I would say the quarters of four of the oranges should be enough. Add these to the pan.

Juice the lemon then pour the juice and water into the pan.

Bring to the boil. Reduce the heat and simmer for 1 to 1½ hours until the rind is very soft and the mixture has reduced by half.

Reduce the heat to low then add the sugar and stir until it has dissolved. Boil for about 10 minutes.

Place a small plate in the freezer and, after 10 minutes, spoon a little of the marmalade onto the chilled plate. If you can draw a line through the marmalade, it is ready. If necessary, cook for a further 5 to 10 minutes and test again.

Let it cool for 5 minutes and then stir in the whisky. Leave it for 10 more minutes before pouring into sterilised jam jars. This will store in your cupboard for six months, but I promise it won't last that long!

HOT TODDY BUNDT CAKE

INGREDIENTS

For the bundt

225g (8oz) butter

225g (8oz) caster sugar

4 eggs

225g (8oz) self-raising flour

1 teaspoon baking powder

2 tablespoons honey

1 lemon, zested

Icing

200g (7oz) icing sugar

3 teaspoons lemon juice

3 teaspoons whisky

(1 teaspoon of cold water at a time if needed to create a runnier consistency)

Nothing beats a soothing mug of hot toddy on a winter's evening – and that inspired me to take those wonderful flavours of honey, lemon and whisky, and combine them into this beautiful Hot Toddy Bundt Cake. A slice of this will definitely ward off those winter blues!

METHOD

Pre-heat your oven to 160°C fan (350°F). Lightly butter your bundt tin (I use a 20cm/8" silicone bundt tin).

Cream together the butter and sugar with a handheld mixer until light and fluffy. Beat in the eggs, one by one, until well combined.

Sift in the flour and baking powder, and stir together carefully on a low speed until just combined.

Add the honey and lemon zest, and mix well.

Place the batter into the prepared tin and bake for 40 to 45 minutes, or until a skewer inserted into the cake comes out clean.

Allow to cool in the tin for 5 minutes, then carefully release the cake onto a wire rack. Leave to cool completely.

To make the icing, sieve the icing sugar into a bowl and begin to mix in the lemon juice and whisky to make a thick but pourable icing. If it isn't runny enough to pour on, mix in a teaspoon of water.

Pour the icing over the cake, scatter over the lemon zest and serve – an accompanying mug of hot toddy is optional!

SHORTBREAD DIPS

MAKES A DOZEN

INGREDIENTS

300g (10½oz) soft butter

125g (4½oz) golden caster
sugar

300g (10½oz) plain flour

50g (1¾oz) cornflour

½ teaspoon fine sea salt

150g (5oz) dark chocolate

150g (5oz) white chocolate

2 tablespoons chopped
pistachios

2 tablespoons freeze-dried
raspberries

There are three traditional ways to serve shortbread – petticoat tails, rounds and fingers. These fingers dipped in chocolate still have the butteriness of traditional shortbread, with that extra indulgence given by the white and dark chocolate. The shortbread biscuit has been made in Scotland for hundreds of years. However, it is widely regarded that it came to prominence thanks to Mary, Queen of Scots. She fell in love with the shortbread served by her French chefs and, from then on, it became the iconic Scottish biscuit we all adore today.

METHOD

Preheat the oven to 150°C fan (340°F). Grease a 20cm (8") square baking tin and line the base and sides with baking parchment.

Cream the butter and sugar in a bowl until pale and fluffy.

Add in both the flours plus the salt and stir until it begins to come together, though take care not to overwork the dough. Bring the dough together with your hands and press the mixture into the prepared tin. Flatten the surface of the shortbread with the back on a spoon and use a fork to prick marks along the length of the fingers.

Bake for 45 minutes until pale golden. Remove from the oven and, with a knife, mark lines where you are going to cut the shortbread. Leave to cool in the tin.

Melt the dark and white chocolate separately in heatproof bowls set over a pan of gently simmering water. Take each of your shortbread fingers and use a teaspoon to coat one third with the chocolate. Sprinkle pistachios or freeze-dried raspberries over the chocolate end and allow to set. Serve with a hot cuppa, or they will keep in an airtight container for up to four days.

HUFSIE

INGREDIENTS

100g (3½oz) soft brown
   sugar

100g (3½oz) butter

1 tablespoon black treacle

150ml (½ cup +
   2 tablespoons) water

200g (7oz) mixed dried fruit

2 eggs

200g (7oz) self-raising flour

1 teaspoon baking powder

2 teaspoons mixed spice

A recipe from the Shetland island of Whalsay, Hufsie is a classic spiced tea loaf. Whalsay is known as the Bonnie Isle, and if you ever visit, keep a lookout during the ferry crossing and you may see why the Vikings called it Hvals-øy – the island of whales. This bake should be served with a thick layer of butter and is perfect for when your auntie comes round for a cuppa and a cèilidh!

METHOD

Pre-heat the oven to 130°C fan (300°F). Butter and line a 900g (2lb) loaf tin.

Into a pan, place the sugar, butter, black treacle, water and dried fruit (you can just use sultanas or raisins if you can't find mixed dried fruit). Simmer the ingredients together for at least 6 to 7 minutes until it turns thick and syrupy.

Allow to cool, then beat in the eggs before folding in the flour, baking powder and mixed spice.

Add the dough to the loaf tin and bake for 45 minutes or until a skewer comes out clean. Cool in the tin and slice to serve.

POSH MINCE & TATTIES

A HEARTY MEAL FOR TWO
— OR THREE IF YOU HAVE A
FRIEND VISITING!

INGREDIENTS

1 onion, chopped

2 carrots, diced

1 parsnip, diced

1 stick of celery, diced

1 tablespoon vegetable or
    olive oil

500g (1lb 2oz) minced
    venison (or steak mince)

2 tablespoons plain flour

100ml (⅓ cup +
    1 tablespoon) red wine

500ml (2 cups) beef stock

1 teaspoon Worcestershire
    sauce

1 heaped teaspoon
    cranberry sauce/jam

Freshly ground black pepper
    and salt

Is there anything more hearty, traditional and Scottish than a bowl of mince and tatties? But I wondered if there was a way to give it an upgrade! Venison is lean, nutritious and sustainable, with lots of flavour. Support your local butcher and ask them to mince the venison for you. For an added twist, I have swapped the classic mashed potato for rumbledethumps, recipe on page 27.

METHOD

Once you have chopped your onion and diced your veg (all to a similar size), add to a large pan with a little oil for about 5 minutes until softened. Then increase the heat, add the mince to the pan and fry until browned.

Reduce the heat, add the flour and stir until combined.

Add the red wine and let it bubble away; it should be absorbed by the mince quite quickly.

Add the stock, Worcestershire sauce, cranberry sauce, salt and pepper.

Stir, then cover and cook for about 45 minutes at a low simmer. If it needs to thicken, remove the lid for the final 5 minutes.

RUMBLEDETHUMPS

INGREDIENTS

400g (14oz) potatoes

300g (10½oz) turnips
(or swede), peeled
and chopped

125g (4½oz) cabbage,
shredded

20g (¾oz) unsalted butter

20g (¾oz) mature Cheddar
cheese

Freshly ground black pepper
and salt

Are rumbledethumps:

a) a side dish

b) the name of a cèilidh band

c) what your head feels like after a night on the whisky

The answer is probably all three! But in this case, a) is the best answer.
Sometimes the side dish takes centre stage and that's definitely the case
with rumbledethumps. This traditional baked dish from the Scottish Borders
of potatoes, turnip and cabbage topped with mature Cheddar will be your
new favourite way to serve veg, and will go perfectly with my Posh Mince
recipe on page 25.

METHOD

Preheat the oven to 160°C fan (350°F).

Peel and chop the potatoes and turnips to similar-shaped chunks and cook
in a pan of boiling water until tender. Drain, season well and mash together
in the pan.

In a frying pan gently fry the shredded cabbage in butter for about
2 to 3 minutes. Add the cabbage to the pan and stir into the mash. Dollop
the mash into an oven dish and grate the cheese on top.

This should be baked in an oven dish for about 40 minutes, taking the lid off
for the final 10 minutes until toasty brown on top. Serve in bowls and feel as
posh as the dish does!

COCK-A-LEEKIE PIE

SERVES 4

INGREDIENTS

1 leek

80g (2¾oz) butter

1 tablespoon flour

300ml (1¼ cups) chicken
stock

10 leaves of tarragon

8 prunes, stones removed

600g (1lb 5oz) boneless
chicken thighs

320g (11oz) packet of
ready-rolled shortcrust
pastry

1 egg, beaten

Salt and pepper

One of the best things about writing a cookbook is choosing and testing all the recipes. This was one of the bakes that hands down was a winner with everyone that tasted it. Take the classic flavours of a cock-a-leekie soup – leek, chicken and prunes – and slow cook them to create this warming and delicious pie. Serve with mashed potato and veg. I promise, it'll become a regular dish served in your kitchen!

METHOD

Chop your leek and add to a pot over medium heat along with the butter until softened. Lower the heat, add the flour and stir together for about 2 minutes before adding your chicken stock a bit at a time to create a smooth sauce.

Chop your tarragon, slice your prunes in half and add them to the sauce. Season with salt and pepper before finally adding your chicken thighs.

This can sit, covered, on a low simmer for about 45 minutes to 1 hour. The sauce should be thick and the chicken soft.

Pre-heat the oven to 160°C fan (350°F).

If you have time, let the chicken mix cool to allow the flavours to enhance before placing into a casserole dish. Lay the shortcrust pastry on top of the pie filling and feel free to add some artistic flair!

Brush the top of the pastry with the egg wash and bake for 40 minutes or until the pastry is golden.

CALEDONIAN CREAM

SERVES **4**

INGREDIENTS

200g (7oz) marmalade

75ml (⅓ cup) whisky

1 orange, juice and zest

20g (¾oz) caster sugar

300ml (1¼ cups) double
cream

Catherine Emily Callbeck Dalgairns (aka Mrs Dalgairns) was a Canadian–Scottish cookbook author born in Charlottetown, Prince Edward Island. First published in 1829, her cookbook *The Practise of Cookery* was written to inspire novice housekeepers to prepare dishes that were in fashion at the time.

I've taken inspiration from her Caledonian Cream recipe (one of the 1,434 recipes in her book!). This is a simple dish that combines wonderful kitchen cupboard Scottish ingredients. Easy to whip up at the last minute for those unexpected guests!

METHOD

In a bowl mix together 100g (3½oz) of the marmalade along with the whisky, juice from the orange, and sugar.

Take a second bowl and whip your cream until peaks appear.

Fold the marmalade mixture into your whipped cream.

Use the additional 100g (3½oz) of marmalade to create a layer to the bottom of each dish, before dolloping your infused cream on top. Serve with a scattering of orange zest.

HEBRIDEAN LEMON CURD

MAKES ONE LARGE JAR

INGREDIENTS

50g (1¾oz) butter

100g (3½oz) sugar

2 tablespoons Isle of Harris Gin

2 lemons, juiced and zested

2 eggs, beaten

Tangy, sharp and a little bit boozy – this lemon gin curd made with Isle of Harris Gin is a real treat. Quicker and easier to make than most jams and marmalades, you can make fruit curds from just about any fruit that can be juiced, but lemon is the most common.

Not only is it delicious on scones, it can be used as a filling for tarts, pies, sponges, whipped with cream into a mousse, or folded into ice-cream.

METHOD

Place a bowl with the butter, sugar, gin, lemon juice and zest over a pan of simmering water. Once combined, slowly add in the beaten eggs, whisking till combined.

Continue to whisk for 10 minutes; it will begin to thicken into a custard texture. You will know when it's ready when you can draw a line through the curd on the back of a spoon.

If you like your curd smooth, pour through a sieve and store in a sterilised jar. It should last 2 to 3 weeks in the fridge.

FLYING SCOTSMAN

SERVES 2

INGREDIENTS

100ml (⅓ cup +
  1 tablespoon) Jura whisky

90ml (⅓ cup +
  1 tablespoon) sweet
  vermouth

1 teaspoon Angostura bitters

1 tablespoon honey

Ice cubes

1 lemon, pared to garnish

Named after the famous steam train, the Flying Scotsman was a cocktail served to the first-class passengers on the train from London to Edinburgh. The original journey in 1862 took 10½ hours, but in 1896 the train was modernised, including the introduction of a dining carriage – serving these tasty drinks. I think a couple of these cocktails and the trip would fly by! Both simple and delicious, this cocktail will make you feel like a first-class mixologist when you master it.

METHOD

Put the whisky, vermouth, bitters and honey in a cocktail shaker with some ice.

Shake well for 20 seconds, then strain into two tumblers filled with ice. Garnish with lemon zest twists and serve.

THE CROFTER &
THE BADGER

The story goes that Murdo Angus, a crofter from the west side of the island, was driving up to Ullapool one early July morning from his daughter's wedding in Oban. From nowhere, a creature ran across the road and slammed straight into Murdo Angus's blue van. In a state of shock, he stepped out of the van to examine what had hit him. Scratching his head, he looked down at a black and white animal he had never seen before, before realising it was a badger – and sadly it was dead.

He stood there crestfallen that he had killed this lovely-looking beast. But Murdo Angus loved to have a story to tell and thought to himself, 'Well, I could take him home so everyone in the village can see it too.' So, he carried the badger into the back of the van and set off for the ferry.

As he arrived home, he saw a fank full of sheep shorn of their fleeces and his three neighbours packing away the wool they'd sheared. He stopped the van and rolled down the window. 'Wait till I tell you what happened to me this morning.'

As he regaled them with a heroic, dramatised story of the morning events, more and more of the villagers began to arrive to find out what all the excitement was. Enjoying having them in the palm of his hand, and all of them captivated by his tale,

his story grew taller and taller – the size of the beast as it attacked the van, the swerve that nearly put him off the road and the thud and the terrible shriek as the poor animal met its demise. They all stood nervously at the back door of the van as Murdo Angus threw the door open.

To Murdo Angus's and the villagers' shock, a very much alive badger jumped out of the van, knocked him to the ground, ran past old Ishbal, who dropped her copy of the *Stornoway Gazette* in the mud, and straight over the hill out onto the moor. The villagers stood around Murdo Angus, speechless. Still on the ground, he whispered to everyone, '*Oh mo chreach*, don't tell anyone!'

The weeks went by and stories began to circulate from the other villages of a mystical beast that was seen on the moor out at night. Some thought they saw a werewolf, others told stories of the return of the *cù-sìth*, a mythological green dog whose howling foretold death to anyone who heard them.

And as for Murdo Angus? Well, he sat by the window of his house every night hoping the folk around the island never found out his part in the story and that the badger sneaked back onto the ferry to Oban!

The craggy coastlines, dark moorland mountains, nooks and crannies of the Hebridean islands are perfect hiding places

for the spirits, monsters and fairies that live amongst us. But it was by the many lochs of the islands that folk saw the most frightening and gruesome of characters.

If you were to take a stroll down to the loch as sun was setting and in the gathering gloom noticed an old woman washing clothes, you might be tempted to go and say hello. This would often be a mistake, for that old woman could be the dreaded *Bean Nighe* – the Washerwoman.

The *Bean Nighe* is regarded as an omen of death and a messenger from the Otherworld. She is a type of *ban-sìth* often found washing the bloodstained clothes of a villager who will die that evening. With her hooked nose and protruding tooth, she was commonly seen wearing a green dress over her frail figure. But meeting her might not be all bad. If you can get between the *Bean Nighe* and the loch before she begins to wash the clothes, she will feel tricked and offer you two options so she can continue her task – she will grant you three wishes or reveal who is about to die. I know which one I would choose!

Though if you are on Islay, be careful not to mix her up with her *ban-sìth* cousin, the *Caointeach*. Every clan on the island was said to have its own *Caointeach*, and when a death was about to occur, she would appear outside the sick person's house wearing a green shawl and begin lamenting at the door. Though less morbid than her counterpart the *Bean Nighe*, she hated to be interrupted at her work and would whip at the legs of intruders with her wet laundry. There was magic and malice in her strike, because those who were hit lost the use of their legs. The moral of this story is, best leave the *ban-sìth* to their scrubbing!

But it wasn't just spirits in the female form that were feared around the islands: *Na Fir Ghorma* were creatures of Hebridean maritime folklore known as the Blue Men of the Minch.

Also known as *Sruth nam Fear Gorm*, the Stream of the Blue Men, the Minch is the water between the Outer Hebrides to the west and mainland Scotland to the east, and is notorious for being a very rough stretch of water to navigate, especially during the strong Atlantic storms that regularly sweep through it.

Na Fir Ghorma were mythological creatures looking for sailors to drown and stricken boats to sink. Though they had the power to create storms, when the weather was fine they would rest floating on the surface of the sea or sleeping in underwater caves. Islanders viewed *Na Fir Ghorma* as helpful if treated with respect. Legend tells of ale being poured into the water as a gift to persuade them to leave seaweed on the beach as fertiliser. Islanders would also light candles by the sea on the night of Samhain to distract the Blue Men from starting their winter storms.

However, like the seas, their mood changed quickly and they could cause ships to founder and their crew perish. To spot a Blue Man in the waves is a sure sign that a storm is approaching. *Na Fir Ghorma* were able to speak, and when they approached a boat that was in trouble they would shout out lines of poetry to the captain and challenge him to complete the verse. If he completed the rhyme successfully, the boat would be spared. If not, then the Blue Men would attempt to overturn the boat and leave its crew to perish in the cold and raging waters of the Minch.

Not all spirit beings can be imposing water creatures, sinister messengers of death or wild unpredictable shapeshifters. Some of the inhabitants of the Otherworld are humble, unassuming and even quite helpful to mortals.

The Urisk was a solitary spirit, said to

be the offspring of unions between mortals and fairies, and had the look of half-man, half-goat. They'd often come down from the mountains in the wintertime to seek shelter in return for performing various chores and tasks. Many farmers were nervous about inviting them in due to their gnarled features, but those who did were rewarded with their work ethic, especially milking the cows, churning butter and cleaning. They worked only during the hours of darkness and accepted small gifts and food in return. It is said that they particularly liked porridge, and also cheese from the dairy. Actually, the more I read about the Urisk, the more we have in common!

Tales of fairies, mermaids, *each-uisge* and other creatures are still told today around fires on the long winter nights, inspired of course by a wee dram or two of whisky. And the next time you drive across the moorlands of Lewis, make sure you keep an eye out for Murdo Angus's badger, just don't tell anyone you know the real story . . .

2
CAKES & BISCUITS

An gog mòr 's an t-ugh beag

The loudest cackle brings the smallest egg

ALMOND & RASPBERRY LAYER CAKE

INGREDIENTS

For the cakes

250g (9oz) butter

250g (9oz) golden caster sugar

5 eggs

½ teaspoon almond extract

175g (6¼oz) self-raising flour

75g (2½oz) ground almonds

For the buttercream

300g (10½oz) butter

600g (1lb 5oz) icing sugar

1½ teaspoon almond extract

For the decoration

40g (1½oz) flaked almonds

150g (5oz) raspberries

For the filling

250g (9oz) raspberry jam

Layers of almond-flavoured sponge topped with raspberry jam and buttercream – this cake has a real wow factor but is deceptively easy to make. Just make sure you allow time for the cakes to completely cool before you slice them and don't be too generous with the buttercream layers as you want to balance the textures and flavours throughout the cake. A bake for sharing with your loved ones.

METHOD

Bake the cake

Preheat the oven to fan 160°C fan (350°F). Grease and line 2 x 20cm (8") sandwich tins with baking parchment.

Cream the butter and golden caster sugar with an electric hand whisk until light and fluffy. Beat in the eggs one at a time, stir in the almond extract then fold in the flour and ground almonds.

Divide the mixture between the two tins, then bake for 20 to 25 minutes until a skewer comes out of the cake clean. Take the sponges out of the oven and leave in the tins for 5 minutes, then transfer onto a wire rack to cool completely. Once cooled, cut each cake into two evenly sliced layers.

Make the buttercream

In a large bowl, cream the butter on its own with an electric hand whisk for about 5 minutes until smooth. Add the icing sugar 200g (7oz) at a time, whisking together between each addition. Finally, add in the almond extract and beat again until smooth.

Decoration

Spread a layer of the raspberry jam on the first of the four sponges and top with a layer of buttercream, place the second layer on top and repeat; same with the third layer. Once you've topped with the fourth layer, spread the buttercream around the sides and top of the cake.

Press the flaked almonds onto the buttercream on the sides of the cake and top the cake with the fresh raspberries.

GINGER PEAR LOAF

INGREDIENTS

The poached pears

1 orange

1 lemon

1 stick of cinnamon

6 cloves

200g (7oz) granulated sugar

500ml (2 cups) water

3 pears (Bosc pears are a
    perfect choice)

The loaf

90g (3oz) soft brown sugar

90g (3oz) butter

90g (3oz) golden syrup

2 teaspoons ginger paste

100ml (⅓ cup +
    1 tablespoon) milk

1 egg

125g (4½oz) plain flour

1 teaspoon ground ginger

½ teaspoon mixed spice

¾ teaspoon bicarbonate of
    soda

Extra handful of plain flour to
    dust pears

The first ever video I shared on TikTok was a Ginger Loaf; it's Peter's favourite of my recipes. I never expected then that I would be creating a new version of the recipe in my second cookbook! This spiced ginger loaf has been given an elegant twist with poached pears. You could also core the pears before you poach them. I use a 450g (1lb) loaf tin for this delicious cake.

METHOD

First, poach the pears. Use a vegetable peeler to peel the zest from the orange and lemon into a saucepan. Squeeze the juice from the orange and pour into the pan.

Add the cinnamon stick, cloves and sugar, pour in the water and bring to a simmer. Cook until the sugar dissolves.

Peel the pears, keeping the stalks on. Then drop gently into the pan, reduce the heat to a gentle simmer for 10 minutes.

Remove from the heat and leave to cool completely on some paper towels.

Now make the loaf. Pre-heat your oven to 160°C fan (350°F).

Into a saucepan add your brown sugar, butter, golden syrup and ginger paste. Stir over a low heat until the butter has melted and the ingredients have combined. Let that cool for 5 minutes.

Stir in your milk and whisk in the egg.

In a separate bowl add your sieved flour, ground ginger, mixed spice and bicarbonate of soda. Make a well in the middle, pour in your wet mixture and combine well.

Dust your cooled pears with some plain flour, then get your lined loaf tin and stand the pears in the tin. If they are particularly rounded, slice off the bottom so they sit perfectly. Pour your cake batter around the pears.

Bake for 30 minutes or until a skewer comes out clean. Leave to cool in the tin for 5 minutes before placing on a wire rack.

Blueberry &
Lemon
Slice

IRENE'S BLUEBERRY & LEMON TRAYBAKE

MAKES 8 SQUARES

INGREDIENTS

For the biscuit base

100g (3½oz) soft butter

50g (1¾oz) caster sugar

150g (5oz) plain flour

For the sponge

100g (3½oz) butter

100g (3½oz) caster sugar

1 lemon, zested

2 eggs

100g (3½oz) self-raising flour

¼ teaspoon baking powder

125g (4½oz) blueberries

For the icing

1 lemon, juiced

135g (4¾oz) icing sugar

Visitors from around the world receive the warmest of welcomes from Irene and her team at the Isle of Harris Distillery café. One of their bestselling cakes is Irene's Blueberry & Lemon Traybake, and I always have a slice when I visit the distillery. Now those of you who can't make it to Tarbert can try it at home!

METHOD

Preheat oven to 170°C fan (375°F). Grease and line an 18cm x 28cm (11" x 7") brownie tin with some baking parchment.

To make the biscuit base, place the butter, sugar and flour into a bowl and beat together to form a firm dough. Add the dough to the brownie tin. Then place another piece of parchment on top and, using the back of a metal spoon, press the mixture down to spread evenly.

With a fork, prick the dough and rest in the fridge for 30 to 60 minutes before baking for 25 minutes until lightly golden.

To make the sponge, cream your butter and sugar together. Add the zest of a lemon and beat in the eggs one at a time. Sieve your flour and baking powder into the bowl and mix together.

Once the biscuit base is baked, leave to cool. Then pour the sponge mixture on top of the biscuit and place the blueberries on top. Bake for 20 minutes or until a skewer comes out clean and the sponge is golden.

For the topping, squeeze the juice of the lemon in a bowl. Sieve in the icing sugar to make a thick, runny icing. Pour on top of the sponge in the tin and let it set before lifting it out using the edges of the parchment.

Slice into squares and share.

EMPIRE BISCUITS

INGREDIENTS

For the biscuit

250g (9oz) softened butter

100g (3½oz) caster sugar

1 egg

½ teaspoon vanilla extract

450g (1lb) plain flour

For the topping

250g (9oz) icing sugar

3 tablespoons milk

Raspberry jam, for spreading

Jelly Tots

Originally known as the *Linzer Biscuit*, these have become an iconic part of any Scottish teatime. Also popular in Northern Ireland, where they are named German Biscuits, these melt-in-the-mouth shortbread biscuits are traditionally sandwiched with raspberry jam and topped with a thick icing. The most important question is – what do you top yours with? A glacé cherry or a Jelly Tot? For me there is no doubt!

METHOD

Cream together your butter and sugar, then mix in the egg and vanilla extract. Sift in the flour in batches and mix well until combined.

Lightly flour a work surface and roll out the dough to a 1cm (½") thickness. Use a round cutter on the biscuits. Place on a baking tray, leaving a bit of space between biscuits to spread. Pop in the fridge for at least 1 hour to firm up.

Preheat the oven to 160°C fan (350°F) and bake for 10 minutes or until baked but still light in colour. Leave to cool completely on a wire rack.

To make the topping, place the icing sugar in a bowl and gradually mix in the milk. Spread the icing on half of the biscuits and spread 1 tablespoon of jam on each of the remaining biscuits. Place the iced biscuits on top of the biscuits with jam. Top each biscuit with a Jelly Tot and share.

HEBRIDEAN BIRTHDAY CAKE WITH PEAT STACK TRUFFLES

For the cakes

150ml (½ cup + 2 tablespoons) single cream

4 tablespoons instant coffee

350g (12½oz) butter, softened

200g (7oz) golden caster sugar

150g (5oz) light brown muscovado sugar

6 large eggs

2 teaspoons vanilla extract

250g (9oz) self-raising flour

1 teaspoon fine salt

For the buttercream

4 teaspoons instant coffee

300g (10½oz) unsalted butter

600g (1lb 5oz) icing sugar, sifted

For the decoration

500g (1lb 2oz) white fondant icing

2 tablespoons apricot jam

250g (9oz) black fondant icing

10g (½oz) red fondant icing

Cocktail sticks

Inspired by a traditional Hebridean thatched house, this birthday cake is layered with coffee cake and coffee buttercream. But no island home is complete without a peat stack, and so these mini chocolate truffles will create an authentic Hebridean scene. As we say in Gaelic, *Meal do Naidheachd* – happy birthday!

METHOD

First, let's make the cakes. Preheat the oven to 150°C fan (340°F). Grease and line two 900g (2lb) loaf tins.

Pour the cream into a small pan and add the instant coffee. Heat gently until the coffee has dissolved and then leave to cool.

Cream together the butter, golden caster sugar and muscovado sugar. It should be light and fluffy (whisk for about 4 minutes).

Beat in the eggs one at a time, followed by the vanilla and cooled coffee cream. Fold in the flour and salt until the batter is smooth.

Evenly measure the batter into the two loaf tins and bake for 40 to 45 minutes, until a skewer comes out clean. Cool on a wire rack.

To make the buttercream, dissolve the coffee granules in 2 teaspoons of boiling water. Beat together the butter and icing sugar. Stir in the coffee and mix until well combined.

To assemble the cake: take the first loaf and slice it in half lengthways. Smooth a generous dollop of buttercream over the lower layer and top with the second layer. Add another dollop of butter on top of the second layer.

To create the roof, slice the edges from the cake to a triangular roof shape – but don't throw away the leftovers! Make a rectangular chimney shape with the leftover cake. You can use some buttercream to mould it together.

Place the roof on top of the first cake and then smother the outside of both cakes in the coffee buttercream.

For the peat stack truffles

100g (3½oz) dark chocolate

75ml (⅓ cup) double cream

15g (½oz) butter

½ tablespoon light brown sugar

Cocoa powder, for dusting

Dust your worktop with icing sugar and roll out your white fondant icing. Cover the whole cake and smooth the fondant onto it.

Gently warm the apricot jam and brush over the roof in preparation for adding the black fondant icing.

Dust the worktop again with icing sugar and roll out your black fondant. This time, only cover the roof shape with the icing, then score lines through the icing. You should have enough black fondant to make two square windows, a doorknob and a chimney pot. Shape a door with the red fondant. Brush the back of each element with apricot jam and place onto the house. Cover your 'chimney' in white fondant and place a round of black icing to make a chimney pot. Use cocktail sticks to hold the chimney in place.

Lastly, make your chocolate truffle peat stack. Chop the dark chocolate into wee pieces. In a saucepan, bring the cream, butter and sugar to a simmer until the sugar has dissolved.

Pour the hot cream mixture over the chocolate and stir gently until melted and smooth. Pour into a shallow dish and chill in the fridge for 3 hours. Slice into small peat-sized squares and arrange into a peat stack by the side of the house. Dust with cocoa powder.

BAA BAA CUPCAKES

MAKES A DOZEN

INGREDIENTS

For the cupcakes

125g (4½oz) butter

125g (4½oz) self-raising flour

1 teaspoon baking powder

125g (4½oz) caster sugar

2 tablespoons milk

2 eggs

1 lemon, zested

For the icing

50g (1¾oz) butter

100g (3½oz) icing sugar

A squeeze of lemon juice

For the sheep

150g (5oz) black fondant icing

15g white fondant icing

120g white mini marshmallows

Kyle and Oscar, my great-nephews, love visiting my brother (their grandad) when he is busy lambing, so these lemon cupcakes with marshmallow wool were a real hit! The zest and juice of the fresh lemon gives these cupcakes the perfect citrusy blast – I think even grandad might like one!

METHOD

This all-in-one method makes for quick easy cupcakes. Preheat your oven to 160°C fan (350°F). Line a muffin tin with paper cases. Put all the cupcake ingredients into a bowl and beat with an electric whisk until evenly combined and smooth.

Scoop the batter into the lined muffin tin and fill each two-thirds full. Bake for 18 to 20 minutes, or until a skewer inserted into the centre comes out clean.

To make the icing, put the butter and half of the icing sugar into a bowl, and beat with an electric whisk until evenly combined and smooth. Add a squeeze of lemon juice (to taste) and the remaining icing sugar, and beat again until light and fluffy. Spread a thin layer of icing over the cooled cupcakes.

To make the sheep: with the black fondant, roll up balls and flatten into a round for the face, then add two wee black fondant triangles for the ears. Place on top of the icing. To make the eyes, take two wee balls of white fondant, flatten them slightly and press them onto the head. Then get two tiny balls of black fondant and press onto the eyes. Add a black fondant tail at the opposite end. Finally, top the rest of cupcake full of white mini marshmallows for the wool.

CARROT & MARMALADE MUFFINS

MAKES 6 MUFFINS

INGREDIENTS

For the cake

100g (3½oz) soft brown sugar

1 egg

1½ tablespoons marmalade

70ml (⅓ cup) vegetable oil

150g (5oz) carrot, grated

50g (1¾oz) dried apricots, chopped to the size of sultanas

½ orange, zested

90g (3oz) self-raising flour

¼ teaspoon bicarbonate of soda

1 teaspoon mixed spice

Pinch of grated nutmeg

Topping

30g (1oz) butter

30g (1oz) icing sugar

60g (2oz) full-fat cream cheese

½ orange, zested

We were sitting by the stove one day with Peter's brother Mark and his fiancée Isla. Tucking into my Carrot & Cardamom Loaf (recipe in my first cookbook), Isla asked, 'Do you think adding marmalade to a carrot cake would work?' Well, I didn't need to be asked twice. I've now baked this as a loaf many times, but I love them as individual muffins topped with a dollop of frosting. Thanks for the inspiration, Isla!

METHOD

Pre-heat your oven to 130°C fan (300°F).

Cream your brown sugar and egg together, then whisk in the marmalade before slowly whisking in the vegetable oil.

Stir the carrot, apricots and orange zest into the batter.

Sift in your flour, bicarbonate of soda, mixed spice and finally some freshly grated nutmeg. Stir together, then divide the mixture evenly into a muffin tin. Bake for 20 minutes, or until a skewer inserted into the centre comes out clean.

Rest in the tin for a couple of minutes before placing on a wire rack.

For the topping, cream your butter for a few minutes. Then sieve in the icing sugar and beat again. Add in the cream cheese and whip until thick and fully combined.

Once the muffins have cooled, top each on with a dollop of frosting and scatter on some orange zest.

JAFFA CAKES

MAKES A DOZEN

INGREDIENTS

For the jelly

1 x 135g orange jelly cubes

1 tablespoon marmalade

150ml (½ cup + 2 tablespoons) boiling water

For the sponge

25g (1oz) caster sugar

1 egg

25g (1) self-raising flour

For the topping

180g (6¼oz) dark chocolate

I know what you're going to say – what's the point in making Jaffa Cakes, the shop-bought ones are delicious! And I agree they are tasty, but homemade ones are on another level! The lightness of that well-whipped sponge alongside the tanginess of the marmalade-infused jelly is the perfect accompaniment to the layer of rich, dark chocolate on top.

And why does the recipe make a dozen? Well, that's how many I can eat in one sitting (without blinking!).

METHOD

To make the jelly, break the jelly cubes into pieces and add into a jug along with the marmalade. Cover with boiling water and stir until the jelly is completely dissolved.

Line a 20cm x 20cm (8" x 8") square cake tin with baking parchment. Pour in the jelly (it should be about 1cm/½" deep) and place in the fridge to set.

Preheat the oven to 160°C fan (350°F). Grease a small bun tin with butter.

To make the sponges, add the sugar and egg to a bowl and whisk together for 5 minutes until light and fluffy. Gently fold in the flour.

Place a heaped tablespoon into each bun tin mould and bake for 7 minutes. Allow to cool in the tin for 3 to 4 minutes before placing on a wire rack.

Using a cookie cutter slightly smaller in size to the sponges, cut rounds from the jelly and place one on top of each sponge.

Melt the chocolate in a heatproof bowl set over a pan of gently simmering water. Then leave to cool slightly and thicken.

Spoon the melted chocolate onto the jelly and, as it is setting, use a fork to create the classic pattern on top.

CHOCOLATE DIGESTIVES

MAKES 16

INGREDIENTS

175g (6¼oz) wholemeal
    flour

175g (6¼oz) rolled oats

150g (5oz) butter, cubed

75g (2½oz) dark soft brown
    sugar

1 teaspoon salt

½ teaspoon baking powder

½ teaspoon bicarbonate of
    soda

2–3 tablespoons cold milk

100g (3½oz) dark chocolate

Digestives get their distinctive flavour from adding wholemeal flour along with the oats and the use of dark soft brown sugar which gives a hint of caramel to the biscuit. Their crunchy texture is in perfect balance with the thick layer of dark chocolate covering the top. You may have eaten these from the supermarket, but I *promise* – homemade is always best.

METHOD

Blend the wholemeal flour and oats together in a food processor until they look like coarse breadcrumbs. Add the butter, sugar, salt, baking powder and bicarbonate of soda and pulse until fully incorporated.

Then, stir in one tablespoon of milk at a time until it comes together.

Wrap in cling film and leave in the fridge for 1 hour.

When ready to bake, preheat your oven on 180°C fan (400°F). Dust the worktop with some wholemeal flour and roll the dough with a rolling pin to a 1cm (½") thickness. Use a round cookie cutter, cut as many rounds as possible with the dough and place on a baking tray with some baking parchment.

Bake for 15 minutes in the oven and leave to cool completely on a wire rack.

Break up the chocolate, add half to a bowl and place in the microwave in bursts of 20 seconds until melted, then add the rest of the chocolate and stir until completely melted.

Cover one side of the biscuits with the chocolate. Allow to cool and share with friends.

BRIOSGAIDEAN SPÌSLIDH

MAKES A DOZEN BISCUITS

INGREDIENTS

Biscuits

225g (8oz) plain flour

175g (6¼oz) demerara sugar

2 teaspoons ground ginger

½ teaspoon mixed spice

1 teaspoon bicarbonate of soda

Pinch of salt

100g (3½oz) cold butter

1 egg

1 tablespoon milk

Buttercream

150g (5oz) salted butter

150g (5oz) icing sugar

The seeds from 2 vanilla pods or 2 teaspoons vanilla bean paste

Life on the croft for my brothers Murdo and Colin and sister-in-law Seonag keeps them very busy, though they definitely don't mind stopping for a cuppa and a treat. I like to think of these as biscuits for grown-ups! These spiced ginger creams have an irresistible crunch and warming flavour. Perfect for sharing, gifting, or solo snaffling!

METHOD

Combine the flour, sugar, ginger, mixed spice, bicarbonate of soda and a pinch of salt. Dice the cold butter and begin to use your fingertips to rub it in until the mixture resembles breadcrumbs.

In a separate bowl lightly beat together the egg and milk. Stir into the dry mixture and bring together into a dough. Cover and chill for 15 minutes.

Preheat the oven to 160°C fan (350°F) and line a baking tray with baking parchment. Take heaped teaspoon-sized scoops of the dough and roll into balls, then place, evenly spaced, on the baking tray. Bake for 12 minutes, until golden. Leave to cool on the tray for 1 minute, then carefully transfer to a wire rack to cool completely.

For the filling, beat together the butter, icing sugar and vanilla until smooth. Spread a thick layer on top of one biscuit and sandwich together with another biscuit.

LEAVING LEWIS

There's a saying in Gaelic: *An diugh aig a' bhuntàt' agus a-màireach ann an Lunnainn* – Today in the potatoes, tomorrow in London. It tells of the adaptability and work ethic of the island folk. We are as comfortable in a pair of wellies, driving a tractor down a one-track road, as we are in a suit running a multimillion-pound business. There is definitely a pioneering spirit amongst the Hebridean people.

I've been lucky enough to have travelled all around the world, and it has amazed me where I have stumbled across people from home. The distinctive lilt in the voices of island folk can never be lost, it doesn't matter how long they have been away. I have sat on a bus in Auckland, queued in a post office in Toronto and drunk a whisky in a New York bar only to hear a fellow *Leòdhasach* beside me.

The first question often asked is 'Cò leis a tha thu?', which translates as 'Who do you belong to?' In practice, island folk often don't use surnames to differentiate (seeing most of us are MacLeods, MacKenzies or MacDonalds!). Instead to try and figure out who you are in the community, we are known by our *sloinneadh* or patronymic. The *sloinneadh* is a way of telling people apart, as well as recalling your family history and being able to figure out how people might be related. They sometimes even mentioned what people looked like, or what their job was.

So if your name was James and your father, Angus, was the son of a red-haired man called James, you'd be Seumas mac Aonghas Sheumais Ruaidh. My *sloinneadh* is Coinneach mac Dhòmhnaill Iain Mhurchaidh an Time. Many an occasion, I've been stopped and asked if I'm related to *an Time*. This was my great-grandfather Angus MacLeod's nickname. He was born in 1854 – it just shows, the apple doesn't fall far from the tree!

When you arrive on the islands on holiday, you may feel like you never want to leave. But two hundred years ago the Outer Hebrides were not the peaceful islands they are today. A melting pot of factors undermined traditional Hebridean society and depressed the island economy, convincing thousands of inhabitants over the years to emigrate en masse to pastures new.

The era of the Highland Clearances was one of the most brutal and heartbreaking episodes in Scottish history. Over the course of 150 years, the islands were changed forever as thousands of families were forcibly driven from their land. Many estates were 'cleared' of their traditional tenant crofters and replaced with livestock like sheep and

deer, which produced higher incomes for the landlords but required far fewer workers. The Clearances took the form of waves of relocations throughout the nineteenth century, where in many cases landlords violently forced tenants to leave their land to reduce the population. In the islands, this often meant abandoning rich farming land on the west coast to scrape a living on the rocky east-coast. Faced with famine and little opportunity to make a living, many took their chance of a place on a departing ship and a new life overseas.

For those islanders on board the *Hector* in July 1773, the decision to leave their native land wasn't an easy one to make. But many looked across the Atlantic hoping for a brighter future. When a Scotsman named John Ross showed up offering a fresh start in Canada, many jumped at this new opportunity.

Ross was a recruiting agent working on behalf of Scottish businessmen in North America. The group had purchased land rights in Pictou, Nova Scotia and charged Ross with finding willing settlers back in Scotland. He was actively encouraged to deceive vulnerable families and use any means necessary to convince people on board. He offered cheap transport and promised supplies and a large piece of coastal farmland to anyone willing to make the journey. Though in reality, all they would arrive to was an uninhabitable inland forest region.

The ship and its cargo of people faced several difficulties throughout the journey. Eighteen people died during the voyage due to the poor and cramped conditions on board. The voyage that was supposed to take six weeks ended up taking nearly double that, meaning that their limited food rations were completely exhausted by the time they docked at Pictou.

When the battered ship and passengers finally arrived, the deception of John Ross became apparent. The supplies and coastal farmland that they had been promised failed to materialise. On top of this, no homes had been built for them and winter was also fast approaching, meaning it was too late to plant any crops to provide food.

To make matters worse, the settlers also quickly found out that the land they were allocated was in a wooded area three miles inland that had yet to be cleared. This meant that they would be unable to fish the coastal waters for food.

Their refusal to take the land caused a backlash from Ross. When the promised supplies eventually showed up, the authorities refused to hand them over. Eventually the stand-off reached breaking point. The settlers refused to take the land that had been allocated to them and set about building homes closer to the shore.

From these dramatic and troubled times, the *Hector* settlers slowly but surely began to make Nova Scotia, and Canada, their new home. Though faced with what must have seemed like insurmountable odds at some times, these intrepid Scottish migrants showed grit and determination. Canada promised them a second chance and a fresh start and they were eager to embrace this opportunity.

Contrary to early waves of emigration, by the 1920s islanders were not driven from their homes by fear of starvation and landlessness, but many did feel that Lewis offered few prospects for the young. The Canadian Government had turned to the Hebrides in its search for domestic servants and farm hands to work in its expanding economy. In contrast, prospects on Lewis were poor and the island still grieved for hundreds of her men who died in the First World War.

Ships had begun sailing direct between Stornoway and Canada and on Saturday, 21 April 1923, the *SS Metagama* sailed from Stornoway with three hundred Lewis emigrants bound for Canada. It was a turning point in the island's history. Within twelve months two more ships, the *Marloch* and *Canada*, departed with more islanders. Some consequences were immediate, such as the sense of loss felt by those returning from their farewells in the town to the village bereft of a son or brother. Other results were slower to make themselves felt: the marriages that would not take place, the children that would not now be born, the homes that would not he built.

Though the impact on the island of those departed has never been forgotten, we continue to be proud of those descended from those families who keep their Hebridean heritage to the fore across the world. Cape Breton is a beacon for Gaelic language and culture and many parts of North America celebrate their Scottish roots with Highland Games and events such as New York Tartan Week around the year. I hope to attend many of these events on my travels across the US and Canada.

If you might be interested in trying to trace family connections to the Outer Hebrides, a great place to start is one of the *Comainn Eachdraidh* or Historical Societies. I recently got my family tree prepared by the team at Seallam. Local legend Bill Lawson has devoted much of his life to tracing the genealogy of the Outer Hebrides, and founded *Cò leis thu?* – Who do you belong to? – a service at Northton Heritage Trust's Seallam centre in West Harris. You never know, we might be related!

3
COSY WEEKEND DISHES

*Thig crìoch air an t-saoghal ach
mairidh gaol is ceòl*

The world may come to an end, but
love and music will last for ever

AUTUMNAL VEG & BARLEY SOUP

SERVES 8

INGREDIENTS

1 butternut squash, about
   1–1.25kg (2–3lbs)

3 tablespoons olive oil

1½ vegetable stock cubes

1 litre (1 quart) water

100g (3½oz) pearl barley

1 onion, chopped

2 garlic cloves, crushed

1 leek, sliced

3 stalks of celery, chopped

2 large carrots, sliced

1 large parsnip, chopped

4 thyme sprigs

Double cream and chilli
   flakes, to serve

Salt and pepper

When does soup season begin? If I see one leaf drop off a tree outside my window – I get my big soup pan out! Autumn's harvest is perfect for soup and really any root vegetables will work in this recipe, so choose your favourites. The addition of pearl barley makes this soup so hearty and filling, perfect to return to after a walk in the hills with Seòras.

METHOD

Preheat the oven to 180°C fan (400°F). Slice the butternut squash into two. Toss with 2 tablespoons of the oil and some seasoning. Lay on an oven tray and roast for 30 to 35 minutes, until tender.

Place the stock cubes and pearl barley in a large pan with 1 litre (1 quart) of water. Bring to the boil and then simmer for 25 minutes. Strain through a sieve over a large jug, top up the stock with water until you have 1 litre (1 quart) again and add the stock to a large soup pan. Place the pearl barley aside.

Heat 1 tablespoon of oil in another pan and gently cook the onion, garlic, leek and celery until softened and add to the soup pan.

Once the butternut squash is ready, remove the seeds, then scoop the flesh into the pan along with the sliced carrots, parsnip, chopped thyme and season well.

Bring the soup to a boil, then simmer for about 45 minutes. Blend the soup until smooth, and finally stir in the pearl barley.

Add a swirl of cream and some chilli flakes sprinkled on top of each warming bowl of soup and serve. This goes perfectly with a slice (or two!) or my Roast Garlic and Courgette Loaf (recipe on page 117).

CULLEN SKINK TART

SERVES *4*

INGREDIENTS

For the pastry

120g (4½oz) plain flour

60g (2oz) cold butter, diced

2 tablespoons iced water

Pinch of salt

For the filling

1 onion

2 potatoes

1 leek

1 tablespoon butter

300g (10½oz) smoked haddock

200ml (¾ cup + 1 tablespoon) milk

1 bay leaf

100ml (⅓ cup + 1 tablespoon) double cream

3 eggs

2 tablespoons chives

Salt and pepper

This is another Scottish soup recipe reimagined: after my Cock-a-Leekie Pie, here comes Cullen Skink Tart. Cullen Skink is a thick Scottish soup made of smoked haddock, potatoes and onions, and these flavours lend themselves perfectly to this tart. To make this an easy weekend dish, you could use a pre-made shortcrust pastry case, but this one is homemade.

METHOD

Sift the flour into a bowl and add the salt. Next add the butter and, with your fingertips, rub it into the flour until the mixture resembles breadcrumbs.

Sprinkle the water over, one tablespoon at a time and, with a knife, work it gently into the crumbs until you have added just enough to form a soft dough, then work into a ball. Wrap and chill in the fridge for an hour.

Roll the pastry out so that it's slightly larger than your 20cm (8") tart tin. Press the pastry into the tin and, with a sharp knife, trim the edges. Prick the base with a fork and chill for 30 minutes.

Preheat the oven to 170°C fan (375°F). To blind bake, line the pastry with greaseproof paper and fill with baking beans or uncooked rice. Bake for 12 minutes until half-cooked, then remove the paper and beans. Return the pastry to the oven for 5 minutes, then leave to cool.

For the filling, chop the onion finely, and the potatoes and leeks into small chunks. Melt the butter in a saucepan over a medium-low heat, then cook the veg gently for about 10 minutes.

Lower the oven temperature to 160°C fan (325°F).

In another pan, poach the fish in the milk with a bay leaf for 5 minutes. Save the milk, then flake the fish and add to the potato and leek mixture.

Pour the poaching milk into a jug and whisk in the cream and eggs. Season well and add the chopped chives.

Place the smoked haddock, potatoes, leek and onion into the pastry case. Pour over the milk till the case is filled and cook for about 30 minutes, until set and toasty brown on top. This is delicious warm but is perfect served cold as part of a picnic.

SAVOURY OAT FLAPJACKS

INGREDIENTS

1 leek, chopped

75g (2½oz) butter

¼ teaspoon smoked paprika

200g (7oz) rolled oats

150g (5oz) carrot, grated

50g (1¾oz) cashews,
roughly chopped

35g mixed seeds (sesame
seeds, sunflower, pumpkin
seeds)

125g (4½oz) mature
Cheddar, grated

50g (1¾oz) Parmesan,
grated

3 eggs

Flapjacks (sorry, American folks – not pancakes, but more like granola bars!) are traditionally sweet, made with golden syrup, dried fruit and nuts. These savoury flapjacks make the perfect brunch or packed in a rucksack and taken on a hike up a Munro for a well-deserved mountaintop treat.

METHOD

In a frying pan, cook the leek in the butter and paprika until the leek has softened, then allow to cool.

Preheat the oven to 170°C fan (375°F).

In a bowl, mix together the oats, grated carrot, cashews, mixed seeds (saving a handful of seeds to top the flapjacks), both the cheeses and the eggs. Combine that all together and then add the softened leeks.

Line a 18cm (7") square tin with baking paper. Tip in the mixture, press down and scatter with the remaining seeds. Bake for 25 minutes or until golden brown. Leave to cool in the tin and then slice for the perfect snack.

CROQUE MADAME ÉCOSSE

SERVES 2

INGREDIENTS

25g (1oz) butter

25g (1oz) plain flour

200ml (¾ cup + 1 tablespoon) milk

200g (7oz) Gruyère, grated

6 slices sourdough bread

1 tablespoon Dijon mustard

2 slices of quality thickly sliced ham

3 thin slices of Stornoway Black Pudding

2 eggs

Oil, for frying

Salt and pepper

The Auld Alliance was signed in 1295 between the kingdoms of Scotland and France. It wasn't simply a military alliance: it was based on a long-established friendship between the two countries. Over 700 years later, I'm bringing the alliance back by taking the best French sandwich and giving it a Scottish twist.

You can find *Croque Monsieur* on most French bistro menus. Add an egg on top to form a *Croque Madame* (the name comes from the look of a woman's hat on top of the sandwich!). I've added a Hebridean layer with sliced Stornoway Black Pudding. Forget the BLT: the CME is the new sandwich in town!

METHOD

To make your béchamel sauce: melt the butter in a pan and add the flour; cook gently for 2 minutes. Add the milk a wee bit at a time and simmer, whisking continuously until thickened. Remove the pan from the heat. Season, stir in 100g (3½oz) of the Gruyère and set aside.

Lightly toast one side of the sourdough bread slices under the grill.

Preheat the oven to 180°C fan (400°F). Spread 2 slices of toast with mustard, spoon on a layer of the béchamel sauce and add a slice of ham to each. Place another layer of sourdough on top of each and spoon another layer of the béchamel before adding a layer of Stornoway Black Pudding. Top with the other toasted bread slices. Spread each sandwich with a large spoonful of béchamel sauce, sprinkle with the remaining cheese and bake in the oven for 10 minutes.

Then turn on the grill again and grill each Croque Madame Écosse for 2 to 3 minutes until the cheese is golden brown.

While your sandwich is grilling, fry 2 eggs in a pan in a little oil. Take your sandwiches out of the oven, top with the fried eggs and serve immediately.

SHONA BARLEY'S HEN & MARAG PIE

SERVES 8

INGREDIENTS

100g (3½oz) butter

500g (1lb 2oz) chicken
  breast, diced

2 rashers of unsmoked
  back bacon (approx.
  110g/4oz)

1 red onion, diced

1 leek, finely sliced

80g (2¾oz) plain flour

300ml (1¼ cups) whole milk

50g (1¾oz) grated
  mozzarella and cheddar
  cheese

Pinch of mustard powder

Season with salt and pepper
  to taste

8 thin slices of Charles
  Macleod Stornoway
  Black Pudding

8 pastry pie shells and lids

When folk ask me what are the three most important sites to visit on the islands, I often say the Callanish Stones, Luskentyre Beach and Charles MacLeod Butchers in Stornoway! For decades, the team at Charlie Barleys have been making not only the best black pudding in the world, but yummy pies and treats served to happy islanders and visitors. Sisters Shona and Ria are at the helm of the shop now and Shona Barley has created the most delicious savoury pie, which of course features their iconic black pudding.

METHOD

Preheat the oven at 160°C fan (350°F).

Melt the butter in a large pan. Add the diced chicken, bacon, red onion and leek. Stir thoroughly until the chicken and bacon have browned and the vegetables softened.

Add the flour a little at a time to avoid lumps forming; we will use this to make a roux. Slowly add the milk to blend with the roux, stirring thoroughly until a sauce is made. Simmer for 20 minutes. Add cheese and stir to thicken, then finally the mustard powder, and season to taste.

Remove the outer skin on the black pudding and place a slice at the bottom of each pie shell. Evenly distribute the chicken and sauce between the pies, then cover with the pastry lids. Bake for 20 minutes.

Serve hot or cold.

MUC MUC

SERVES **4**

INGREDIENTS

For the batter

125g (4½oz) plain flour

¼ teaspoon fine sea salt and
 black pepper

2 eggs

175ml (¾ cup) milk

75ml (⅓ cup) cold water

For the pigs

6 rashers bacon

6 pork sausages

3 tablespoons vegetable oil,
 plus a little extra for frying

I still have no idea why Pigs in Blankets are only allowed at Christmas. Along with mincemeat, I am planning a petition to make these yearlong food celebrations! Until then, I am tucking my well-wrapped pigs into a classic Toad in the Hole recipe. Could this be the greatest crossover of two wonderfully named dishes ever? Muc is the Gaelic for a pig – and this dish is double the pig and double the love.

METHOD

Prepare the batter at least an hour before cooking. Sift the flour and salt into a mixing bowl and grind in some black pepper. Break in the eggs and start to whisk together. Combine the milk and water together in a jug and slowly add to the batter, whisking all the time. You should be left with a smooth batter. Cover and place in the fridge for an hour.

Preheat your oven to 200°C fan (425°F).

Add your rashers of bacon into a hot frying pan – you just want to give them some colour, but they will cook in the oven. Wrap each sausage with a rasher of bacon.

Add 3 tablespoons of oil to a medium-sized roasting tin and place in the oven for 7 minutes, at which point the oil should be smoking hot. Pour the chilled batter into the roasting dish. Arrange the bacon-wrapped sausages on top.

Quickly place the roasting tin back in the oven and cook for 30 minutes. It should rise well and have crispy edges. Be careful not to open the oven while it's cooking, curiosity killed the cat and might make your batter collapse!

Serve with onion gravy, mashed potatoes and curly kale.

SLOW COOKED BEEF CHEEK CASSEROLE

INGREDIENTS

For the casserole

1 large onion, chopped

4 sticks celery, chopped

2 cloves garlic, finely sliced

Bunch of fresh thyme, stalks removed

2 carrots, chopped into chunks

2 beef cheeks

400ml (1⅔ cups) red wine

600ml (2½ cups) beef stock

1 teaspoon redcurrant jam

Olive oil, for frying

Finishing touches

Fresh sourdough loaf

2 cloves of garlic

1 carrot

Handful of curly kale

Support your local butcher! With names like shin, cheek and flank, the cheapest cuts of meat can sound severe and a little intimidating. However, butchers know the worth of these less popular cuts – they often have far more flavour than their expensive counterparts. By ordering the two cheeks, you will have a hearty meal for four.

However, these cuts do generally require longer cooking, so take advantage by using them in casseroles – perfect for a cosy weekend dish! As an extra treat, serve this casserole in a hollowed-out sourdough and let all that red wine gravy soak into to the bread.

METHOD

Pre-heat the oven to 100°C fan (250°F).

In a large casserole dish, gently fry the onion and celery in olive oil over a low heat until they start to soften. Add the garlic, thyme leaves and the carrots.

Place the beef cheeks in the dish and pour over the red wine. Allow that to get to a bubbling simmer for a couple of minutes before adding the beef stock and redcurrant jam, making sure the cheeks are fully immersed. Season well and cover with a lid, then place the dish in the oven and slowly braise for 5 to 6 hours, or until incredibly tender.

When you take the dish out of the oven, turn up the heat to 180°C fan (400°F). Slice the top off the sourdough. Pull chunks out of the bread and place them in an oven dish, brushed in olive oil, with a couple of cloves of garlic for 8 to 10 minutes or until they get crispy edges.

Chop up your carrot and add to a pan of boiling water. After 3 minutes, drop in a handful of kale and simmer for another three minutes. Drain and stir into the casserole.

Ladle the casserole into to the sourdough loaf and serve along with your chunky croutons.

FISHERMAN'S PIE

INGREDIENTS

1 onion, chopped

1 leek, chopped

1 chilli, chopped (optional)

240g (8½oz) smoked haddock

240g (8½oz) cod loin

750ml (3 cups) milk

1 bay leaf

300g (10½oz) baby potatoes

50g (1¾oz) butter

50g (1¾oz) plain flour

75g (2½oz) frozen peas

3 boiled eggs, sliced into quarters

Handful of fresh parsley

5–6 ready rolled sheets of filo pastry

3 tablespoons melted butter to brush on the pastry

As the son of a fisherman, I can't have a cookbook without a fish pie! This rich pie packed with cod, smoked haddock, leeks and peas has a crispy filo pastry top that adds crunch to the soft filling. If you like, you can prepare the filling in advance and simply place in the oven when you layer on the filo. Perfect for when family and friends pop by.

METHOD

Add your chopped onion, leek and chilli into a large frying pan with a little oil and soften over medium heat.

Meanwhile, put the haddock and cod in another pan, cover with the milk and add the bay leaf. Cook gently for 5 minutes, or until just tender. Remove the fish from the pan with a slotted spoon (reserving the milk), transfer to a plate and leave to cool slightly.

Add your potatoes to a pan of salted water and boil until they are partially cooked, then drain and leave aside.

When your vegetables have softened in the pan, stir in the butter and flour, and cook gently for 2 minutes. Slowly add the reserved milk to blend with the roux, stirring thoroughly until the sauce is made, and take off the heat.

Slice the potatoes in half, add them to the pan along with the flaked fish and frozen peas, and gently stir together.

Preheat the oven to 180°C fan (400°F).

Take a large pie dish, pour in the filling, lay the quartered boiled eggs over the filling and scatter the fresh parsley on top. Brush each sheet of pastry with melted butter and lightly scrunch it up. Place on top of the pie and repeat with the remaining sheets. Bake for 30 to 40 minutes, or until the filling is piping hot and the pastry is golden brown.

FISH FINGER SANDWICH WITH HOMEMADE BAKED BEANS

INGREDIENTS

For the baked beans

100g (3½oz) pancetta, chopped

1 onion, finely chopped

1 garlic clove, finely chopped

400g (14oz) can chopped tomatoes

1 tablespoon dark muscovado sugar

1½ tablespoons cider vinegar

200ml (¾ cup + 1 tablespoon) cold water

400g (14oz) tin of cannellini beans

For the fish fingers

40g (1½oz) panko breadcrumbs

2 tablespoons desiccated coconut

250g (9oz) haddock fillet

70g (2½oz) plain flour

2 eggs, beaten

Olive oil, for frying

To serve

Fresh sourdough bread

Butter

Mayonnaise

Tartare sauce

Rocket leaves

My father had a trawler fishing boat when I was growing up: its name and number was SY313 Ripple. Because my village was too far away, I had to board at school in Stornoway. Every Tuesday and Thursday night, I would wait for the boat to land its catch at Stornoway pier. On a Thursday, Dad would give me money to go to the chippie and get a fish supper – what a treat. Now, as a treat I make this. Both are so easy to make, it's the perfect comfort food.

METHOD

To make the baked beans, add olive oil to a saucepan over medium heat, then add the pancetta and allow to cook for 3 minutes before adding the onions and cooking for a further 5 minutes. Stir in the garlic, tomatoes, sugar, vinegar and 200ml (¾ cup + 1 tablespoon) water, allow to come to a boil and add the cannellini beans. Reduce the heat to low and cook for 1 hour, stirring occasionally, until your sauce has thickened.

Meanwhile begin to make your fish fingers: combine the breadcrumbs with the desiccated coconut and season well.

Cut the haddock into fingers. Coat each finger in the flour, then dip into the beaten egg and finally roll in the breadcrumb mixture until evenly covered on all sides.

Add some olive oil to a frying pan on a medium heat. Add the haddock fingers and fry for 2 to 3 minutes on each side, until crisp, golden and cooked through.

Take 4 thick slices of sourdough bread and smother in butter, mayonnaise or tartare sauce – or all three! Add some rocket and then 2 of your fish fingers per sandwich. Serve with a side of your baked beans.

SPEEDY SMOKED KEDGEREE

SERVES 4

INGREDIENTS

1 tablespoon olive oil

1 onion, peeled and finely
chopped

2 cloves garlic, peeled and
finely chopped

1 small piece fresh root
ginger, peeled and finely
chopped

1 tablespoon medium curry
powder

½ teaspoon ground
coriander

½ teaspoon ground turmeric

250g (9oz) basmati rice

500ml (2 cups) vegetable
stock

300g (10½oz) smoked
haddock fillets, skinned

2 handfuls frozen peas

3 eggs

Kedgeree is a fuss-free brunch dish of spiced rice, smoked haddock, eggs
and peas – it is warm and comforting with a soothing seafood flavour that
can be rustled up and on the plate in half an hour.

METHOD

Heat the oil in a heavy based saucepan. Add the onion, garlic and ginger
and cook gently for 7 minutes.

Add the curry powder, coriander and turmeric and cook for a minute or two
more.

Add the rice and the vegetable stock; cover and cook for 10 to 12 minutes.

Cut the fish into chunks, add to the rice and cook for another 5 minutes.

Take off the heat, stir in the peas and leave to stand, covered, for 5 minutes.

At the same time, soft boil the eggs.

Cut the eggs into quarters, scatter over the rice and serve.

'SE UR BEATHA

My father had two favourite radio shows that he never missed. Every Sunday before he took his crew out to fish the Atlantic waters around Lewis he'd listen to *The Shipping Forecast* on Radio 4, and Friday nights wouldn't have been the same in our house (and nearly every other house on the islands) if the laughter, stories and tunes of Neen MacKay and Iain Mac 'ille Mhìcheil's show *Na Dùrachdan* weren't playing from the wireless in the kitchen.

If you wanted to find out what was happening on the island, you didn't listen to the news, but instead switched on *Na Dùrachdan*. As every wedding, anniversary and ninetieth birthday was announced – usually with my father announcing in a surprised tone '*Shaoil mi gun robh e marbh!*' ('I thought he was dead!') to the radio – Neen introduced a classic song from The Lochies, a ceilidh tune from Donald MacRae or Fergie MacDonald playing the accordion. *Na Dùrachdan* is a big, cosy hug of a radio show and all these years later it is still on every Friday night. I just hope someone will request a song for my ninetieth birthday!

We're always tuned to Radio nan Gàidheal as we drive through the island – be it Cathy MacDonald with *Naoi gu Deich* and *A' Mire ri Mòir* with Mòrag Dhòmhnallach in the mornings, Seonag Monk in the afternoons with *Caithream Ciùil* or Mairead NicIllinnein presenting *Tiompan* on Friday evenings, her voice is like velvet! Along with an amazing group of other personalities, Radio nan Gàidheal brings Niall Iain, Derek Pluto, Emma, Megan, Eilidh, Mark and many more to our homes around the world.

It was on Sunday 2 December 1923 that the first Gaelic radio broadcast was heard. A fifteen-minute-long religious message by Reverend John Bain from King's College in Aberdeen came across the airwaves. Two weeks later, Gaelic was back on the radio, this time with Christmas songs being performed. But it wasn't until October 1952 that the first television broadcast was in Gaelic. The performances of Gold Medallists Anne Gillies and Donald MacLeod, as well as the Lovat and Tullibardine champions Glasgow Gaelic Music Association, were filmed at the Grand Concert that concluded the Royal National Mòd held in Rothesay.

Things began to change on 2 December 1964 when Calum Kennedy hosted *'Se Ur Beatha*, the first ever Gaelic light entertainment show on the BBC. Calum was born only a few miles away from my village of Cromore in Orinsay on the Isle of Lewis. After being presented the Gold Medal at the 1955 Mòd by Queen Elizabeth II, he became known as the 'Voice of the Highlands', performing

Gaelic songs across the country. He even won the 1957 World Ballad Championships representing Scotland at the Bolshoi Theatre in Moscow and was presented with his award by the then Soviet leader Nikita Khrushchev.

The story goes that at his peak he was such a household name that, in 1963, when headlines screamed 'Kennedy shot', distraught islanders assumed it was their favourite singer, rather than the US president, who had been assassinated.

Taking part in that first programme with Calum were fellow islanders Kathleen, Peggy, Agnes and Fiona, collectively named The Macdonald Sisters, along with Calum Ross, The Islands Group, led by Flora MacNeil from Barra and two old favourites, Iain Darroch and Lachie MacLean.

By 1972, 'Se Ur Beatha was regularly being watched by over 800,000 viewers – ten times the amount of Gaelic speakers in the country. That series was the first to be recorded and transmitted in colour, much to the excitement of the Aberdeen *Evening Express* newspaper who wrote the page three headline, '*Gaelic fans' new series go gay in colour*'! Calum Kennedy was joined by three other hosts – Anne Lorne Gillies, Kathleen MacDonald (who had sung with her sisters on the first show) and Alisdair Gillies. And at the height of its success, it was moved to the primetime BBC 1 Saturday evening slot between *Sportreel* and Michael Parkinson's talk show.

But if you ask anyone in Scotland what their favourite Gaelic TV show was – they will all say *Dòtaman*!

Dòtaman, meaning spinning top, was a long-running Gaelic kids' TV show featuring music, learning and puppets. It was fronted by folk musician Donnie MacLeod, who, along with his sister Mairead, had sung in the Gaelic supergroup Na h-Òganaich. Each week Donnie wore a funny hat (and you were wondering where I got that idea from!) to sing songs – including the iconic '*An tractar a th' agamsa*' – and get puppets Nelson and Napoleon to tell him the time. He became so synonymous with the show that he is still know as *Donnie Dòtaman* all these years later.

Another presenter on the show was Cathy MacDonald, undoubtedly the Queen of Gaelic Radio and Television. Originally from Uig on the Isle of Lewis, she has presented on every genre from politics to music, history to travel. It would be impossible to imagine her dulcet tones and warm laughter not coming out of your radio each day. Or to watch the BBC Alba Hogmanay show without her wishing you *bliadhna mhath ùr*. But even more so, presenting coverage from the Royal National Mòd. It was there in 2018 that I met Cathy for the first time. Pàdruig and I had just won the duet competition and were whisked off to sing live on her show. As we were waiting in the wings, Cathy came up to say congratulations and give us both a big hug. I must admit, I was starstruck! Since then, I've been lucky enough to appear on many of her programmes and meet her at events – and I'm still starstruck every time!

The most momentous change in Gaelic broadcasting came when BBC formed a partnership with MG Alba and announced that a dedicated Gaelic channel called BBC Alba would launch. The channel began at 9 p.m. on 19 September 2008 with a video featuring a new rendition of the Runrig song 'Alba' sung by the stars of Gaelic music and TV. The first programme was a live cèilidh from the Isle of Skye, presented by Mary Ann Kennedy.

I've been lucky enough to have featured on programmes about baking, learning Gaelic, Hogmanay, gardening and music

– they have always been so much fun, and being around other folk who are passionate about Gaelic has been so special. Most evenings we'll sit down to watch one of the wonderfully created shows on BBC Alba, be it *Gàrradh Phàdruig*, *Trusadh*, *Fuine*, *Seòid a'Chidsin*, *Eòrpa*, *An Lot* or *Mach à Seo*. And even if you don't speak Gaelic, tune in – there are subtitles for most of the programmes and you'll definitely enjoy it!

But there is one show I would love to watch the re-runs of, and that is the nineties kids programme *Dè a-nis*, hosted by none other than Pàdruig! In his seven years on the show, he went on rollercoasters at Disney, made gargoyle door knockers for Halloween, interviewed pop group S Club 7 and buried a time capsule, amongst many other adventures! Actually, I've thought of a new series I'd definitely like to see – Pàdruig and Seòras riding rollercoasters around the world, what do you think BBC Alba?!

4
BREAD & SCONES

Gabh uabhar a bhiadh-maidne le pailteas, a dhìnnear le gainne agus a shuipear le mì-chliù

Eat breakfast like a king, lunch like
a prince and dinner like a pauper

CROFTER'S LOAF

INGREDIENTS

500g (1lb 2oz) strong plain white bread flour, plus extra for dusting

7g (½oz) fast action dried yeast

2 tablespoons olive oil, plus extra for oiling

1 teaspoon fine salt

350ml (1½ cups) lukewarm water

1 teaspoon sea salt flakes

If you're a busy crofter or a bread-making novice, this loaf is perfect. All the work is done by the dough while you are sleeping! There is no kneading, fancy equipment or techniques required, and with a bit of preparation the day before, you will have a delicious, freshly baked loaf ready for lunchtime.

METHOD

Begin preparing your bread the day before you wish to enjoy it. Add together the flour, yeast, olive oil and fine salt in a bowl and mix together. Pour in the water and combine together with a knife to form a dough. Oil some cling film, cover the bowl and place in a warm kitchen to rise for at least 14 hours.

The next morning, the dough should have doubled in size and the surface will be covered in bubbles.

Dust the work surface with flour, then flour your hands. Gently scoop out the sticky dough into a rough circle on the flour, trying not to knock out too much air. Pull the edges of the dough into the middle to bring it together in a rough ball shape.

Turn the dough over and place on a large square of floured baking paper so the folded edges are underneath. Tuck the dough around itself to make a ball. Sprinkle with some sea salt flakes then lightly dust the top with flour. Cover with clingfilm and set aside somewhere warm for an hour.

Heat the oven to 200°C fan (425°F). Put an empty casserole dish with the lid on into the oven for 30 minutes. Once the casserole dish is hot and the dough has proved, transfer the dough, still on its baking paper, to the casserole dish. Replace the lid, put in the oven and bake for 40 to 45 minutes.

Remove the lid from the casserole dish and bake the bread for another 25 minutes until the crust is golden and the bread sounds hollow when tapped on the base. Cool on a wire rack, slice and serve.

CATHY BHÀN'S ISLAND SCONES

MAKES 4

INGREDIENTS

225g (8oz) plain flour, plus extra for dusting

½ tsp bicarbonate of soda

1 teaspoon cream of tartar

30g (1oz) cold butter, cubed

2 teaspoons golden syrup

1 large egg

60ml (¼ cup) buttermilk

Pinch of salt

I think this might have been my favourite day in putting this book together – baking in Cathy MacDonald's kitchen, what a treat! As a fellow islander, Cathy shares a love for old family bakes and every island kitchen needs a great scone recipe. What would be better than sitting in your kitchen listening to Cathy's show on Radio nan Gàidheal and tucking into one of these homemade treats?

METHOD

Preheat the oven to 200°C fan (425°F).

Sieve the flour, salt, bicarbonate of soda and cream of tartar into a large mixing bowl. Add the butter, then rub in with your fingers until the mix looks like fine crumbs.

Add the golden syrup, egg and buttermilk, and combine together gently; I use a cutlery knife for this.

Scatter some flour onto the work surface and tip the dough out, then fold the dough over 2 to 3 times until it's a little smoother. Pat into a round shape about 5cm (2") deep. Slice into four.

Scatter some more flour on a baking sheet lined with parchment and place the scones closely together.

Bake for 12 minutes. Cool slightly on a wire rack and serve warm. Perfect with butter and jam!

OAT & CARROT ROLLS

INGREDIENTS

350ml (1½ cups) lukewarm water

2½ teaspoons fast-action dried yeast

450g (1lb) strong white bread flour, plus extra for dusting

½ teaspoon sea salt

65g (2oz) rolled oats

1 tablespoon olive oil

120g (4oz) grated carrot

These bread rolls are a combination of softness from the dough and sweetness from the carrots. The oats give it a rustic texture. They are perfect to serve with a bowl of hearty soup for lunch.

METHOD

Stir the water and yeast together in a large mixing bowl until the yeast has dissolved. Add 350g (12½oz) of the flour and the salt, mixing quickly to form a dough. Turn out onto a lightly floured surface and knead well for a couple of minutes. Add the oats and oil, and continue to knead. Add the carrots and the remaining 100g (3½oz) of flour, and knead for an additional few minutes until the dough is soft and pliable. Sprinkle with a bit of extra flour, cover with a clean tea towel and let rise in a warm kitchen for an hour, until doubled in size.

Punch down the dough on a lightly floured surface and divide into four portions. Divide each portion into three pieces and roll each piece into a ball, flattening them slightly. Dust lightly with flour and arrange on two lined baking sheets. Cover with a tea towel and let rise for 30 minutes.

Meanwhile, preheat the oven to 180°C fan (400°F). After they have proved, bake the rolls for 15 minutes until they have risen and are golden brown.

BROCHAN BREAD

INGREDIENTS

200g (7oz) cold leftover porridge

300ml (1¼ cups) lukewarm water

500g (1lb 2oz) strong white bread flour, plus extra for dusting

½ tablespoon caster sugar

2 teaspoons sea salt

7g (½oz) dried yeast

Small handful of oats, to sprinkle

Oil, for greasing

I love porridge, I eat it every day. But even after all these years, I still haven't perfected portion control! So every so often I have some leftover porridge. If this happens to you, don't throw it out – it makes the perfect ingredient in this simple bread recipe. It makes the loaf extra rich, with a terrific crust and a chewy, moist texture to the crumb.

METHOD

Add the porridge into a bowl with the water. Stir in the flour, sugar, salt and yeast until combined. Cover with a damp tea towel and leave to prove for 1 hour; it should double in size.

Tip the dough out onto a lightly oiled surface and knock it back. Then fold and knead for a minute.

Shape the loaf and, with the seams of the dough at the bottom, transfer to an oiled 900g (2lb) loaf tin and scatter the top with a few oats. Cover with the damp tea towel and rest for a further 45 minutes.

Preheat the oven to 200°C fan (425°F).

Slash the top with a sharp knife and place in the oven. Bake for 10 minutes, then turn the heat down to 170°C fan (375°F) and cook for a further 30 minutes until golden brown. The loaf sounds hollow when tapped. Cool on a wire rack.

WILD GARLIC SCONES

MAKES 4

INGREDIENTS

225g (8oz) self-raising flour

1 teaspoon baking powder

100g (3½oz) chilled butter, cubed

125g (4½oz) mature Cheddar cheese (or Parmesan), grated

30g (1oz) wild garlic, washed and finely chopped

100ml (⅓ cup + 1 tablespoon) milk

1 egg

Peter and I love going foraging, be it wild brambles for jams, gorse flowers for cocktails or hazelnuts for chocolate spread. With its fresh garlicky smell, wild garlic is the unmistakable scent in woodlands in spring. Wild garlic has a softer flavour to traditional bulb garlic, and the green, pointed leaves are easy to identify and pick. It makes great pesto, but I love to bake these wild garlic scones along with a tasty, strong cheese. Just make sure you have lots of salted butter to serve with this savoury treat.

METHOD

Preheat oven to 200°C fan (425°F) and line a baking tray with baking paper.

In a bowl, combine the flour and baking powder. Then add the butter and use your fingertips to rub it into the mixture until it resembles coarse breadcrumbs.

Add 100g (3½oz) of the cheese and the wild garlic and mix until combined.

Pour in the milk a little at a time and mix with a knife. Only use enough milk until a dough forms.

On a floured surface, shape into a round and flatten to 2.5–3cm (1") thick. Use a cookie cutter to stamp out rounds and place them on a lined baking tray. Brush the top of each scone with egg and sprinkle over with the remaining cheese, before placing in the oven for 13 to 15 minutes until golden brown on top.

Cool slightly on a wire rack, then smother in salted butter.

ROAST GARLIC & COURGETTE LOAF

INGREDIENTS

1 garlic bulb

4 medium-sized courgettes

500g (1lb 2oz) strong white
  bread flour

1½ teaspoons salt

2 teaspoons fast-action dried
  yeast

225ml (¾ cup +
  3 tablespoons)
  lukewarm water

2 tablespoons olive oil

Olive oil and sea salt to
  season

My sister-in-law Seonag is famous for her courgette loaf with roasted garlic. After years of pleading with her for the recipe, I can finally share it! I can't stress enough, get every little bit of liquid out of the courgettes that you can. The smell as the bread is baking will make you swoon. Try your best to let it cool a little before slicing up and smothering in salted butter.

METHOD

Pre-heat the oven to 180°C fan (400°F). Cover the garlic bulb loosely in foil, place on a baking tray and roast for about 30 to 35 minutes.

Grate the courgettes, place in a tea towel or muslin cloth and, with all your might, squeeze the liquid out. Once you think you've got it all out, squeeze again!

Place the flour and salt in a bowl, making a well in the centre. Stir the yeast into a teaspoon of the lukewarm water and add into the well along with the rest of the water and the olive oil. Mix together until the dough begins to come away from the sides of the bowl.

Flour your work surface and knead the dough for 5 to 7 minutes. It should become smooth and elastic. Place in an oiled bowl which has been covered with a damp tea towel for an hour. It should double in size.

Remove the roast garlic from the bulb and mix in with the courgettes.

Knock back the dough and begin to knead again while adding the garlicky courgettes.

Once it has combined together, brush with olive oil and sprinkle on sea salt. Cover and leave to prove for an hour.

Pre-heat the oven to 180°C fan (400°F). Bake the loaf on a lined baking tray for 25 minutes. It should be golden and hollow sounding when you tap the bottom. Leave to cool slightly, slice and serve with a bowl of soup (like my Autumnal Veg & Barley Soup, page 76).

BLACK STOUT SODA BREAD

INGREDIENTS

200g (7oz) wholemeal flour

250g (9oz) plain flour

15g (½oz) bicarbonate of
soda

150g (5oz) rolled oats

1 teaspoon salt

250ml (1 cup) black stout

1 tablespoon black treacle

1 tablespoon honey

250ml (1 cup) buttermilk

Vegetable oil, for greasing

Soda bread is a quick bread that does not require any yeast or time to prove. Instead, all of its leavening comes from bicarbonate of soda and buttermilk, and you will have a delicious loaf of bread on the kitchen table in an hour. You can use your favourite stout; mine is the Dark Ness Rich Black Stout from the Loch Ness Brewery (no monsters were harmed in the making of this stout). This full-bodied stout adds a delicious flavour that pairs well with the whole grains. The loaf is hearty and goes well with stews and soups, but it is equally tasty served simply with butter and smoked salmon.

METHOD

Preheat the oven to 200°C fan (425°F) and grease a 900g (2lb) loaf tin with vegetable oil.

Into a bowl, add your wholemeal and plain flour, bicarbonate of soda, oats and salt; mix together. Pour in the stout, treacle, honey and buttermilk. Mix well to form a wet dough.

Tip the dough onto a lightly floured work surface. Roll and fold the dough gently and place in your loaf tin.

Bake for 15 minutes, then turn down the oven to 170°C fan (375°F) and bake for a further 35 to 40 minutes. Cool on a wire rack.

CRUMPETS

MAKES 6 CRUMPETS

INGREDIENTS

150g (5oz) plain flour

200ml (¾ cup +
   1 tablespoon) water

½ teaspoon salt

½ teaspoon sugar

1 teaspoon baking powder

1 teaspoon dried yeast

Making homemade fluffy crumpets is so satisfying. Crumpets are crisp on the bottom, soft and chewy on the top, and delicious from every angle! A classic treat, seen first in Elizabeth Raffald's 1769 cookbook *The Experienced Housekeeper*. Always eat warm, allowing the butter to melt through the holes. To make sure you get the signature holes topping your crumpets: don't rush the resting time, don't have your pan too hot and if you don't get them to work the first time – try, try and try again!

METHOD

Add the flour, water and salt to a mixing bowl and whisk until you get the consistency of double cream – this will take a few minutes.

Mix a tablespoon of water into your yeast.

Add the sugar, baking powder and yeast mixture to bowl and mix for another minute.

Cover the mixing bowl and rest in a warm kitchen for an hour.

Place a few greased metal cookie cutters onto a griddle or non-stick frying pan on a medium heat.

Spoon about 4 tablespoons of batter into each ring (to three-quarters full). Cook for 5 minutes, or until little bubbles appear on the surface.

Once the bubbles have burst, leaving little holes, carefully lift off the rings and flip over the crumpets, then cook for 1 minute on the other side.

Place on a wire rack to cool slightly. Serve warm (or toasted) smothered in butter.

THE COINNEACHS

'And what's the name?' said the girl behind the counter holding a polystyrene cup in her hand. 'Coinneach,' I said, smiling politely after ordering myself a mint tea. She looked at the cup, and with a bemused expression, scribbled something with her felt-tip pen and shouted 'Next!' at the old lady behind me.

A moment later, a hot takeaway cup was thrust in my hand with the word 'Kanye' written on it. This undoubtably would be the first and most likely the last time I would ever be mistaken for an American hip-hop rapper. There is no question, the name Coinneach will leave some intrigued, many confused, but most asking, '*What did you say?!*'

In history, there have been kings, clan chiefs and even a saint named Coinneach. St Coinneach was born at Glengiven in Ulster in 515 and when he was fifty he joined St Columba on Iona. There are writings which attribute miracles of the wind and sea to Coinneach and he had two churches dedicated to him on South Uist: Cill Choinnich at Àird Choinnich and another at Beinn Ruigh Choinnich. But there is one Coinneach from the Isle of Lewis that is definitely the most heralded.

It was a summer's evening in the early seventeenth century, and a lady from Uig on the west coast of the island had taken her cattle up to graze the pastures on the side of a ridge called Cnoceothail, which overlooks the graveyard at Baile-na-Cille. She sat outside a sheiling, a wee stone bothy, where she had lit a fire.

At midnight, she looked over to the church and gasped as she saw hundreds of spirits rising from their graves and begin to go in all directions – over the hills, down to the village and setting sail over the seas. The woman hid in the doorway of the shieling waiting to see what would happen next. One by one throughout the night, the spirits began to come back. And as they did, their graves would close behind them. But there seemed to be one grave that sat open for many hours after the others had returned.

Nervously, the woman began to walk down the hill towards the churchyard. In her hand was a *cuigeal*, a tool used for spinning wool. She remembered a story her mother had told her that said a spirit could not return to their grave if a *cuigeal* was laid upon it.

She did not have to wait long, as from the north she saw a beautiful fair-haired lady coming towards her. The lady called out, 'Lift thy *cuigeal* from off my grave, and let me enter my dwelling of the dead.' Nervously the woman replied, 'I shall do so when you explain to me what detained you so long.'

The lady nodded and began: 'My journey was much longer than theirs – I had to go

all the way to Norway. I am a daughter of the King of Norway; I was drowned off the coast of my country, but my body washed up on these shores and was found on the beach close to where we now stand, and I was then interred in this grave.'

As the woman began to walk towards the grave to pick up the *cuigeal*, the princess said, 'In remembrance of me, and as a reward for your courage, walk over that hill and head for the loch. Beside the large rock, you will find a blue stone. Take this home and give it to your son.'

The woman lifted the *cuigeal*, and the princess was laid to rest again.

By the time she had reached the loch, the sun had begun rising over the hills. There by the rock, as the princess promised, was a wee blue stone with a hole through the middle of it. She collected her cows and hurriedly took the path back to the village.

Her son Coinneach was gathering sheep as she returned. 'Coinneach, I have a gift for you,' she said as she handed him the hagstone and told the story of the previous night. He lifted the stone to his eye and a shaft of light from the sun shone through the hole in the middle. He immediately began to see visions through the stone and realised these were events that had not yet happened.

These prophesies returned to him day and night. Soon, what he saw through the stone began to come true. People in the village called him a *taibhsear,* a visionary. They named him Coinneach Odhar, the Brahan Seer.

An dà shealladh is the Gaelic for 'the two sights'. This gift was seen in men, women and children, and would allow them to see visions of the living – it was very rare for those with *an dà shealladh* to be able to see people beyond the grave. This gift was often passed down in families, and when a child was born with one blue eye, and one brown,

it was a good indication that they would have the sight.

Having become famous for his predictions and charm, Coinneach began working for Kenneth Mackenzie, the 3rd Earl of Seaforth. But, unfortunately for the Seer, the accuracy of his predictions were to be his downfall.

While the Earl was away in Paris, his wife Isabella called for Coinneach Odhar and asked him to tell her how her husband was. The Seer seemed reluctant to give much information at first and simply said that he was in good health. This incensed Isabella, who demanded the truth. The Seer then told of her husband's infidelity with a French lady, much fairer than herself. This was all too much for Lady Isabella, and she flew into a rage and called for the guards.

When it became apparent that there would be no mercy for Coinneach, he pulled out his stone and used it one last time. His chilling prediction was a curse on the family of MacKenzie: '*The line of Seaforth will come to an end in sorrow. The last Earl will be both deaf and mute and follow his four sons to the grave.*'

When the Brahan Seer had finished his prophecy, he took his stone and cast it into the loch, before Lady Isabella had poor Coinneach thrown into a spiked barrel of tar. What a way to go.

Three generations passed after the death of Coinneach Odhar before the prediction came true. In 1783, Francis Mackenzie inherited the title of Earl. He was indeed deaf and mute due to contracting scarlet fever in childhood. Francis' four sons all died before he did, fulfilling the final prophesy.

Such is the belief in Coinneach's prophecies that to this day he is still influencing the course of history. The Seer predicted that when there were five bridges over the River Ness, there would be worldwide chaos. In

August 1939, the fifth bridge over the river was completed and two weeks later Germany invaded Poland and World War Two began.

In another prediction he was walking on the moor when he said, '*Thy bleak wilderness will be stained by the best blood of the Highlands. Glad I am that I will not live to see that day where heads will be lopped off in the heather and no lives spared.*' Half a century later the infamous Battle of Culloden was fought on that spot.

Fortunately there is one of Coinneach's predictions that has yet remained untrue. He told that the island of Lewis will be laid waste by a destructive war. One that would continue till the rival armies, slaughtering each other as they went, reached Tarbert in Harris. The battle for Lewis would only be won if a left-handed MacLeod called Donald, son of Donald, son of Donald led the army to victory. Let's all hope that Coinneach was looking through the stone upside down that day and it will never come to pass.

So, be it St Coinneach, King Coinneach, Clan Chief Coinneach, Coinneach Odhar or humbly Coinneach, the Hebridean Baker – just don't call us Kanye.

5
AFTERNOON TEA RECIPES

Is miosa brochan gun salann,
na balach gun fheusag

Porridge without salt is worse than a
young man without a beard

BRADAN RÒST PÂTÉ ON BLINIS

MAKES 16 SERVINGS

INGREDIENTS

For the blinis

100g (3½oz) strong bread flour

70g (2½oz) plain flour

1 teaspoon fast-action yeast

¼ teaspoon of salt

250ml (1 cup) lukewarm milk

1 egg

Olive oil, for frying

For the pâté

200g (7oz) full-fat cream cheese

1 tablespoon crème fraîche

½ lemon, juiced

150g (5oz) hot smoked salmon (bradan ròst)

Small bunch dill, chopped

Salt and pepper

Bradan Ròst is the Gaelic for roast salmon. It is made by dry curing salmon fillets with salt and sugar, then hot smoke and kiln roasting. The flavour is delicious, and for me, a real step up from traditional smoked salmon. This quick pâté is full of flavour and perfect to top these homemade blinis.

METHOD

Blinis

Add the bread flour, plain flour, yeast and salt into a bowl. Into a jug, add the warm milk, whisk in an egg and pour into the flour mix.

Whisk together until there is a smooth batter. Cover the bowl with cling film and leave to stand for about 1 hour.

Heat a large non-stick pan with some olive oil. Use a teaspoon to drop in the batter and make mini pancakes. Cook for about 90 seconds, until bubbles appear on the surface of the pancakes. Flip over and cook for another minute. Place on a wire rack to cool.

Pâté

Into a food processor add the cream cheese, crème fraîche and lemon juice, season well with salt and black pepper, then give it a blitz. Flake the bradan ròst into the food processor and pulse a few times. I like it chunky, but the longer you pulse the smoother it will get.

Stir in some the chopped dill, spoon into a bowl and sprinkle the remaining dill on top. Serve on top of your homemade blinis.

STORNOWAY SCOTCH EGGS

MAKES 4

INGREDIENTS

6 eggs (4 for soft boiling,
  2 beaten)

6 quality pork sausages
  (about 300g/10½oz)

275g (10oz) Stornoway
  Black Pudding

Plain flour, enough to fill a
  bowl

Bowl of panko breadcrumbs

Vegetable oil, for deep frying

Salt and pepper

Adding the rich, well-seasoned flavours of Stornoway Black Pudding
to your sausage meat makes these the tastiest Scotch eggs you'll ever
have. Many folk think these will be challenging to make, but with minimal
preparation and making sure you are safely deep frying, you will be
rewarded with a hearty snack. Perfect warm or cold.

METHOD

To get the perfect soft-boiled egg, lower 4 eggs into a pan of boiling water
for 7 minutes. Have a bowl of ice-cold water ready and drop them in
immediately to halt the cooking process. You can peel them once they have
cooled.

Remove the sausage meat from the skins and add along with the black
pudding to a bowl. Season well with salt and black pepper, mix together
and then split into four equally sized portions.

Take one of your portions, flatten it out in your hand and wrap evenly
around an egg.

Have three bowls ready: one with plain flour, one with 2 beaten eggs and
one with breadcrumbs. Dip the Scotch eggs into the flour, then the egg
mixture, then the breadcrumbs.

Half-fill a saucepan with vegetable oil and heat until it reaches 180°C
(350°F) on a thermometer. Frying two Scotch eggs at a time, cook for
8 minutes until golden and crisp, turning occasionally, and rest on some
kitchen paper.

Make sure the thermometer still reads 180°C (350°F) before adding the
next two eggs.

LEMONADE SCONES

MAKES 6

INGREDIENTS

350g (12½oz) self-raising
   flour, plus extra for dusting

150ml (½ cup +
   2 tablespoons) double
   cream

150ml (½ cup +
   2 tablespoons) sparkling
   lemonade (e.g. Sprite)

1 lemon, zested

Pinch of salt

1 egg, beaten

Fluffy, moist and so easy to make, these Lemonade Scones are so quick to prepare. Yes, I do still love a traditionally made scone, and who doesn't want that buttery flavour that comes from them. But honestly, when I serve these – no-one notices! Don't expect the lemonade to make them taste of lemons, but I couldn't resist adding some lemon zest.

METHOD

Preheat the oven to 200°C fan (425°F).

Add the flour, cream and lemonade to a bowl along with the zest of a lemon and a pinch of salt, and mix until just combined. Take care not to overwork the dough.

On a floured surface, shape the dough into a round and flatten to 2.5–3cm (1") thick. Use a cookie cutter to stamp out rounds and place on a lined baking tray. Brush the top of each scone with egg before placing in the oven for 13 to 15 minutes.

Cool on a wire rack. When ready to serve, I take the Cornish tradition of jam then cream. You can dollop on raspberry jam or, in keeping with the lemon theme, spoon a layer of homemade lemon curd (see page 32 for the recipe) and top with cream or clotted cream.

BAKEWELL SCONES

MAKES 6

INGREDIENTS

350g (12½oz) self-raising
    flour

1 teaspoon baking powder

40g (1½oz) sugar

95g (3oz) cold butter, cut
    into cubes

50g (1¾oz) marzipan,
    grated

50g (1¾oz) chopped glacé
    or maraschino cherries,
    chopped in three

150ml (½ cup +
    2 tablespoons) milk

2 teaspoons almond extract

1 egg, beaten

2 tablespoons flaked
    almonds

There is one ingredient in this recipe that takes these scones to the next level – grated marzipan! I didn't want the almond flavour to just come from the extract (though I recommend Pure Almond Extract from Nielsen Massey, it is beautifully fragrant), so adding the marzipan gave these scones that frangipane flavour you want from a Bakewell tart. This has very quickly become my go-to scone recipe.

METHOD

Into a bowl add the flour, baking powder, sugar and butter. Use your fingers to rub the butter in until it resembles breadcrumbs. Add the marzipan and cherries.

With a knife, slowly stir in the milk and almond extract into the flour mixture, then use your hands until just combined, taking care not to overwork the dough.

On a floured surface, shape the dough into a circle, flatten to 2.5cm (1") thick and chill in the fridge for about 30 minutes.

Pre-heat the oven to 200°C fan (425°F).

Use a cookie cutter to stamp out rounds and place these on a lined baking tray. Brush the top of each scone with egg, sprinkle over the flaked almonds and bake in the oven for 13 to 15 minutes.

Cool on a wire rack. These are delicious served with cherry jam and cream.

CHURCH WINDOW CAKE

SERVES 6

INGREDIENTS

For the sponge

125g (4½oz) butter, softened

125g (4½oz) caster sugar

2 eggs

½ teaspoon almond extract

100g (3½oz) self-raising flour

50g (1¾oz) ground almonds

2 teaspoons milk

Red food colouring (I use Dr Oetker's gel food colouring – nearly the whole tube)

Pinch of salt

To cover

100g (3½oz) apricot jam

350g (12½oz) marzipan

Icing sugar for dusting

Better known by its classic name, the Battenberg Cake, it makes me smile that this has this wonderfully named alter-ego. This almond-flavoured cake has a real taste of nostalgia.

METHOD

Heat oven to 160°C fan (350°F). Using a triple layer of foil, make a barrier down the centre of a 20cm (8") square tin, then line each compartment with two pieces of baking parchment.

To make the sponge, cream the butter then whisk in the sugar a couple of tablespoons at a time.

Whisk the eggs and add the almond extract. Gradually beat this into the butter mixture.

Sift in the flour, salt and ground almonds into the bowl. Finally, add the milk and carefully fold everything together with a metal spoon. Measure half the mixture and place in another bowl. Add the food colouring into one of the bowls until you get a real vibrant pink batter. Carefully spoon the uncoloured mixture into one half of the tin and level the top, then spoon the pink one into the other half and do the same. Bake for 20 to 25 minutes, until a skewer comes out clean. Allow to cool for a couple of minutes then turn out onto a rack.

Cut each sponge in half lengthways so you end up with two pink and two yellow strips.

Warm the apricot jam in a saucepan with a tablespoon of water then press through a sieve. Take a pink cake and brush one side with the jam. Place a yellow piece next to it, jam sides together, and push gently together. Brush the top surface with jam and place a piece of yellow cake atop a pink piece and vice versa. Brush all the outside edges with more jam.

Knead, then roll out your marzipan on a surface dusted with icing sugar into a 30cm x 20cm (12" x 8") rectangle, large enough to wrap the cake.

Roll the cakes up tightly in the marzipan, gently smoothing the marzipan with your hands to neaten it up. Turn back over with the seam underneath, trim a slice off each end and serve.

GIN BABAS

SERVES 6

INGREDIENTS

For the babas

220g (7½oz) strong bread flour

7g (½oz) sachet fast-action yeast

½ teaspoon salt

50g (1¾oz) sugar

70ml (¼ cup + 1 teaspoon) milk

2 eggs

100g (3½oz) melted butter

For the syrup

250g (9oz) caster sugar

200ml (¾ cup + 1 tablespoon) water

4 tablespoons gin

For the Chantilly cream

1 vanilla pod, seeds only

100g (3½oz) icing sugar

250ml (1 cup) double cream

To serve

Raspberries and a dusting of icing sugar for garnish

Traditionally soaked in rum, this delicious mini French cake with an Ukrainian name deserves a Hebridean twist with gin from the Isle of Harris Distillery.

These benefit from being made a day in advance, so when it's time to soak in the gin-infused syrup the babas devour every drop.

METHOD

Into a bowl add the flour, then place the yeast on one side of the bowl and the salt on the other side. Add the sugar and stir everything together.

Whisk together the milk and eggs. Add half of this mixture to the flour and combine, then mix in the rest. Then add the melted butter.

Turn the dough out onto a worktop and knead for 10 minutes. Place in a bowl, cover and allow rise for about an hour – it should double in size.

I use a medium-sized six-hole silicone savarin mould, which are about 5–6cm (2") across. Lightly grease each of the moulds.

Turn the dough out of the bowl and knock it back by kneading it a few times. Add the dough into a piping bag and fill the six moulds.

Preheat the oven to 160°C fan (350°F).

Allow the dough to prove again until it has expanded almost to the top of the mould. Then bake for about 20 to 25 minutes.

To make the syrup, put the sugar in a small saucepan with 200ml (¾ cup + 1 tablespoon) water and bring to a boil. Simmer for 5 minutes, take off the heat and add the gin.

Allow the babas to cool a little in the moulds before placing them on a wire rack. Drop the babas into the saucepan of syrup one at a time, carefully turning them (or spoon over the syrup) to make sure they soak it up. Give them at least a minute each.

For the Chantilly cream, scrape the seeds of a vanilla pod, add to a bowl with the icing sugar and cream, and whip until it holds its shape. Pipe the cream on top of the babas, top with raspberries and dusted icing sugar.

ÙISDEAN'S CHOCOLATE-TOPPED DUFFS

INGREDIENTS

To make the duff

225g (8oz) plain flour, sieved

1 teaspoon baking soda

1 teaspoon mixed spice

1 teaspoon cinnamon

175g (6¼oz) caster sugar

100g (3½oz) suet

100g (3½oz) sultanas

75g (2½oz) currants

75g (2½oz) raisins

1 apple, grated

150ml (½ cup + 2 tablespoons) buttermilk

1 egg, beaten

1 heaped tablespoon black treacle

Pinch of salt

The topping

200g (7oz) white chocolate

200g (7oz) dark chocolate

Peter and I appeared on the BBC Alba Hogmanay special of the cookery show *Seòid a' Chidsin* with hosts Ùisdean and Roddy Angus, the kitchen coves. It was a bake by Ùisdean that really caught my eye (and tastebuds). His twist on a classic clootie dumpling (or duff, as we say in Gaelic) was to slice and top each bite with chocolate. It won me over immediately and I think it'll do the same for you.

METHOD

To make the duff, sieve your flour into a large bowl and add your baking soda, mixed spice, cinnamon, sugar, suet, dried fruit, grated apple and salt into a bowl and combine.

Pour in your buttermilk, beaten egg and black treacle. Stir together.

Dip a piece of muslin cloth or a cotton dishtowel (the cloot) in boiling water for 15 seconds, remove and once cool enough to touch, ring the cloth out. Place the cloth on your work surface and sprinkle liberally with flour.

Place the mixture into the centre of the cloot. Gather up the edges of the cloth and tie it up (not too tightly) with string, leaving some room for the dumpling to expand.

In a large pan of boiling water (enough to cover the dumpling), place a saucer upside down. Place the dumpling onto the saucer, cover with a lid and simmer for 3 hours. Top up the water if necessary.

Take out from the pan and carefully remove the cloot from the dumpling, trying not to take off any of the skin.

In a warm kitchen, let it rest until cooled and the skin has formed. Slice your duff whichever way you like.

Melt the chocolates separately in heatproof bowls set over a pan of gently simmering water and once they have cooled slightly, spoon over the top of the sliced duff and leave to set on a wire rack.

COINNEACH'S TEA CAKES

MAKES 6

INGREDIENTS

For the chocolate domes
400g (14oz) dark chocolate

For the biscuits
50g (1¾oz) plain flour

50g (1¾oz) wholemeal flour

½ teaspoon baking powder

25g (1oz) caster sugar

25g (1oz) butter

1 tablespoon milk

For the marshmallow
3 egg whites

150g (5oz) caster sugar

6 teaspoons golden syrup

½ teaspoon vanilla bean paste

As a Scottish baker, there are a few recipes you need in your arsenal: shortbread, clootie dumpling, tablet and cranachan for starters. And tea cakes definitely need to go on that list!

Here are my top tips for great tea cakes: 1. Slowly melt your chocolate, it will stop it discolouring when it sets; 2. Don't overfill your chocolate domes with marshmallow; 3. For an extra retro twist, dollop a teaspoon of raspberry jam in the middle of the biscuit before you assemble.

METHOD

First, prepare your silicone dome moulds with chocolate. Melt 300g (10½oz) of chocolate in a heatproof bowl over a pan of gently simmering water. Spoon the chocolate into each mould, moving it around with a spoon to cover the mould completely. Leave to set (but not in the fridge).

Preheat the oven to 150°C fan (340°F).

For the biscuits, add both flours, baking powder and sugar to a bowl. Rub in the butter with your fingertips. Add the milk and stir together into a ball.

Roll out the dough on a floured work surface to 5–10mm thickness and use a cookie cutter slightly smaller than the chocolate dome to cut out the biscuits. Place on a baking tray and chill in the fridge for 15 minutes.

Bake for 10 minutes and cool on a wire rack.

Take the remaining 100g (3½oz) of your chocolate and melt it in a heatproof bowl set over a pan of gently simmering water, then dip one side of the biscuits. Place the coated biscuits onto the wire rack to set.

Add the egg whites, sugar, golden syrup and vanilla to a bowl and sit on a pan of simmering water. Whisk until it looks silky and doubles in size. Normally it takes me 7 minutes with an electric hand whisk. Place the marshmallow into a piping bag.

Get the chocolates out of the silicone moulds, and pipe in the marshmallow, filling them nearly to the top. Take a biscuit, press onto the marshmallow and lay biscuit-side down on the wire rack until completely set.

LEMON TARTLETS

INGREDIENTS

For the tartlets

150g (5oz) self-raising flour

15g (½oz) ground almonds

45g (1½oz) icing sugar

75g (2½oz) cold butter, cubed

2–3 tablespoons milk

For the filling and topping

175ml (¾ cup) lemon curd

125g (4½oz) mascarpone

2 lemons, zested

½ orange, zested

1 tablespoon orange juice

2 tablespoons icing sugar

There's definitely a lemon theme to this afternoon tea! This recipe from my sister-in-law Seonag makes buttery mini tarts filled with sweet and tangy lemon curd and creamy mascarpone, and they are melt-in-the-mouth delicious.

METHOD

Add the flour and ground almonds into a bowl, then sift in the icing sugar.

Add the butter, then rub in with your fingers until the mix looks like fine crumbs.

Use the milk to bind together to make a soft dough. Knead lightly and chill for 30 minutes.

Pre-heat the oven to 160°C fan (350°F).

Roll out the pastry thinly. Use a medium-sized cookie cutter to cut 12 pastry rounds and place them in a tartlet tray, pressing into the tartlet shape.

Add a heaped teaspoon of lemon curd into each tartlet and bake in the oven for 8 to 10 minutes, until the edges are golden.

Meanwhile, mix the mascarpone, the zest of one lemon, the orange zest and juice, and the icing sugar together. Once the tartlets are cooled, dollop this mixture on top. Sprinkle the zest from the remaining lemon on top of each.

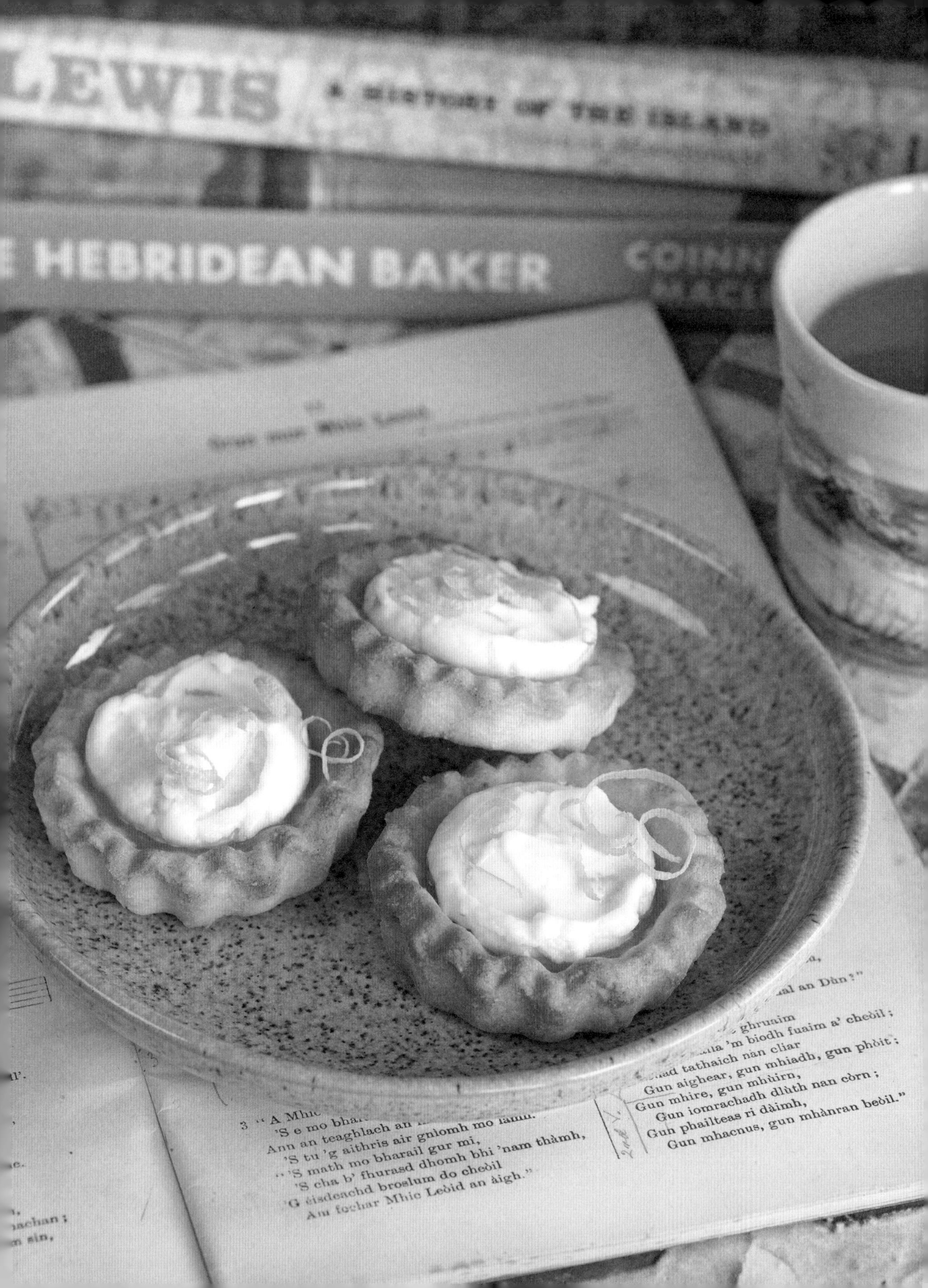

LEMON CURD COCKTAIL

INGREDIENTS

90ml (⅓ cup +
   1 tablespoon) gin

60ml (¼ cup) freshly
   squeezed lemon juice

20ml (1 tablespoon) sugar
   syrup

2 teaspoons lemon curd

Lemon rind, to serve

Originally from the Argyll town of Dunoon, Iona has the wonderful task of promoting the Isle of Harris Distillery around the world and has Hebridean connections through her grandmother, who is from the Isle of Barra.

Iona's apéritif is so easy to assemble. The lemon curd adds creaminess to this sweet and tangy gin cocktail, which will be a perfect accompaniment to an afternoon tea or as a welcome drink for friends coming round for a cèilidh.

METHOD

To make the sugar syrup, add 200g (7oz) of caster sugar and 100ml (⅓ cup + 2 tablespoons) of water into a saucepan and simmer over a low heat until the sugar has dissolved. Cool completely. You can store it in the fridge for up to a month.

Into a cocktail shaker add the gin, lemon juice, sugar syrup and lemon curd. Shake to combine, then add a handful of ice and shake again.

Serve in chilled martini glasses with a lemon rind spiral.

THE HERRING GIRLS

If you look closely at the coat of arms of Stornoway, you'll see how its people and the seas have been so influential on the town. The colours recognise the three families who have had the most influence on the island: the MacLeods, the MacKenzies and the Mathesons. Along with the castle, the two symbols in the shield represent a ship and the most important fish to the island – the herring.

My father, brothers, uncles, grandfathers and the generations before them worked as fishermen. But this story talks of the women in my family and how the seas changed their lives, for better and for worse.

My granny, Anna Sheonaidh, was born in Marvig on the Isle of Lewis in 1900. Growing up, there were very few employment opportunities available to the women on the islands, and so along with nearly two thousand other local women, every season she would travel from Stornoway to Lerwick in the Northern Isles, through Wick and Peterhead, to as far south as Yarmouth and Lowestoft in England, following the fleets of fishing boats as one of the Herring Girls.

She would pack up all her possessions, including clothes, oilskins, rubber boots and bedding into a *ciste* or wooden chest and set sail on the Stornoway–Kyle of Lochalsh mail steamer. Then they took a train bound for one of the east coast fishing ports. The boat and the train echoed to the sound of Gaelic singing and stories of the girls as they caught up on the news from the other villages around the island.

Island women were used to hard work and although herring gutting entailed long hours for a low wage, they cheerfully gave a good account of themselves. For that reason they were popular with their employers and the other workers involved in the herring trade.

The Herring Girls worked in crews of three girls. Two of them were gutters and the third, usually the tallest, was a packer. She packed the gutted herring in tiers of salt in barrels. The dexterity of the girls gutting and packing the herring had to be seen to be believed. The routine was for the girls to be woken up at 5 a.m. by a cooper banging at their door and calling, 'Get up and bandage your fingers.' With a swift twist and turn of the wrist, the herring were gutted at the rate of thirty to fifty herring a minute, hour after hour all day, so the chances of cutting their fingers was very high. Over a cup of tea, the girls tied bandages round their fingers in order to avoid being nicked with the special sharp knife they used to gut the herring called a *cutag*. Actually, when Queen Elizabeth II visited Stornoway in 1956, she was presented a golden *cutag* inscribed with the town's

motto, *God's Providence Is Our Inheritance*.

The reward was hardly commensurate with the hard labour that was expected from these young islanders and they would return from a whole season away with only £10 to £12 in their pockets. And although the Herring Girls were on the whole fairly easy going, it is known that they once participated in a strike in Yarmouth in order to improve their pay from tuppence to one shilling a barrel. Mounted police were brought up from London to intimidate the girls but they would not be provoked; rather they continued their good-humoured bantering, Gaelic singing and laughing. After a week, they gained their full demand for a shilling a barrel and the police and their horses humbly returned to London.

The girls were employed six days a week, but when Saturday evening arrived and the fishing boats were in port, the island boys were ready for a cèilidh. An accordion and fiddle were always found and Gaelic songs were heard from the ports all along the coastline.

The Herring Girls are now commemorated by two statues on the harbourside in Stornoway and every family on the island will have heard stories of their granny or great-granny's adventures.

But as my granny Anna came back from the herring for the final time, she wasn't to know that those seas that brought so much laughter and friendship would also cause so much pain and sadness to her and the family.

In the summer of 1961, Anna's two sons, Kenny and Seonaidh, travelled to Carradale in Argyll to buy *The Maimie*, a crab fisher boat. After arriving back home in Marvig, they took their new boat out and fished the waters around the island.

As summer turned to winter and storms began to gather, life out at sea got harder. On

Wednesday, 31 January 1962, my mother, Ciorstaidh Anna, who was only nineteen at the time, stepped onto *The Maimie* at Stornoway harbour with her brother Kenny and cousin Seumas. It was about eight in the evening and they planned to sail the nine nautical miles back to the family home in Marvig.

They had not travelled far when the engine began to fail, and as the storm began to pick up, *The Maimie* drifted onto the Sgeir Mhòr at Inaclete. The worsening weather stopped the Stornoway lifeboat and the anti-submarine frigate *HMS Malcolm* from getting near and all they could do was watch the boat with my mother, her brother and cousin drift towards the rocks.

The ordeal suffered by the crew in the seven-and-a-half-hour struggle for survival on that stormy, freezing night has gone down in the annals of maritime history of this seafaring community as a night of profound tragedy and epic heroism. Despite being badly injured while breaking out of the wheelhouse where the crew were trapped, Seumas jumped into the stormy waters from the rocks in an attempt to swim towards a floating lifeline, and to the heartbreak of his cousins on board, he perished in the attempt.

At 3.30 a.m., the Stornoway lifeboat finally got close enough to all that remained of *The Maimie* above the surface of the water and rescued Kenny and Ciorstaidh Anna. They were both taken to the Lewis Hospital frozen stiff and suffering from exposure.

The tight-knit fishing communities of these islands know only too well that the seas can bring blessings or change fates forever. And as they arrived home to their mother, my granny Anna, they grieved the passing of their cousin Seumas. The village and island were left heartbroken by his death.

Over the years, the island's bards have

written stories and poems about the sea. The tragedy of *The Maimie* is remembered in verse to this day.

THE MAIMIE

One dark and stormy winter's night The
  Maimie left the pier,
She was homeward bound for Marvig and
  the lighthouse seemed so near.
When all at once the engine failed and
  they were swept ashore,
On to that treacherous Battery Rock the
  locals call Sgeir Mhòr.
Now the crew of three looked round
  prepared to meet their doom,
A sudden light rose in the sky shone on
  them like the moon.
They knew their plight was known help
  wasn't far away,
For they could see the Stornoway lifeboat
  coming towards them over the bay.
And there upon the Battery shore the
  lightboat stood by,
With breeches buoy and rockets they
  would win the fight or die.
And the lights of HMS Malcolm shone
  brightly through the sky,
Showing everyone aboard The Maimie
  high and dry.
Then a fellow called Mackenzie jumped
  down onto the rock
To retrieve a dangling lifeline the rescuers
  had shot.

He didn't make it first attempt but the
  second time he won,
Then suddenly a wave crashed down and
  Mackenzie he was gone.
They could see him swimming for his life
  towards the Sandwick shore,
On the shore they prayed for that brave
  lad till they could see him no more.
But the other two aboard as calm and
  brace could be,
With the man aboard the lifeboat trying
  to save them from the sea.
The lifeboat moved in slowly near to the
  Maimie's side,
And those on board were taken off despite
  the rising tide.
They were taken safely back to shore the
  night now nearly gone,
But they had many a bitter tear for their
  friend who had gone before.
Now we always will remember in silent
  sympathy,
Of the tragedy that happened there on the
  angry sea.
It's not so easy to forget that disastrous
  hour,
When the gallant vessel grounded on the
  treacherous Sgeir Mhòr.

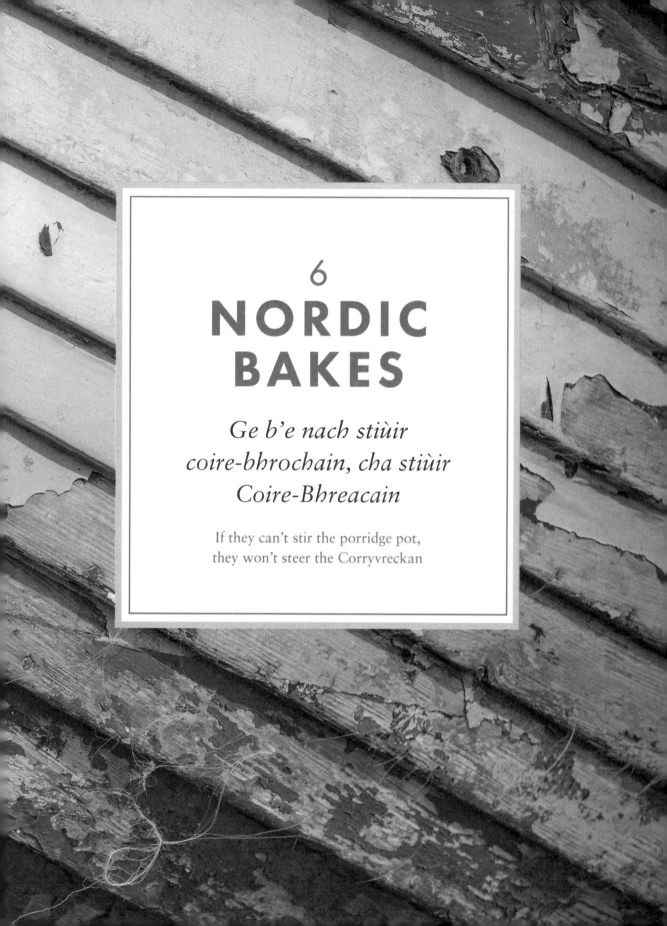

6
NORDIC
BAKES

*Ge b'e nach stiùir
coire-bhrochain, cha stiùir
Coire-Bhreacain*

If they can't stir the porridge pot,
they won't steer the Corryvreckan

ROMKUGLER

INGREDIENTS

500g (1lb 2oz) Madeira cake (actually any cake will work; even better if it's a bit stale)

3 tablespoons raspberry jam

80g (2¾oz) icing sugar

100g (3½oz) butter, softened

3 tablespoons cocoa powder

3 teaspoons rum essence (or for an adult treat use real rum; you might need to add another teaspoon)

For decoration

Chocolate vermicelli, desiccated coconut or cocoa powder

Imagine throwing away cake? Sacrilege! But this was a challenge faced by some Danish bakers when closing their bakery one day, when they had pastries and cakes which would not be fresh enough to be sold the day after.

Instead of throwing them out, the bakers decided to give them a makeover. And the result was a huge success! Combining the cake with store cupboard ingredients, they rolled them into balls and sold them decorated in chocolate sprinkles. Queues of adults and kids snapped up these cheap wee treats, which quickly became a Danish tradition.

METHOD

Time to get your hands dirty! Crumble up the cake into a bowl, add the jam, icing sugar, softened butter, cocoa powder and rum essence and mix together with your hands (or a wooden spoon or a standing mixer) until evenly combined.

Depending on which cake you use, you might need to add a wee bit more cocoa or rum. Or you might like to add rolled oats for a wee bit of texture. Trust your taste buds!

Place in the fridge for 30 minutes then begin to roll the dough into balls.

Roll each ball in chocolate vermicelli, desiccated coconut or cocoa powder. Chill in the fridge and take them out 10 minutes before serving.

KVÆFJORDKAKE

INGREDIENTS

For the cake

150g (5oz) butter

150g (5oz) caster sugar

4 egg yolks

4 tablespoons whole milk

1 teaspoon vanilla extract

150g (5oz) plain flour

1 teaspoon baking powder

Pinch of salt

For the meringue

4 egg whites

Pinch of cream of tartar

200g (7oz) caster sugar

100g (3½oz) flaked almonds

**For the crème pâtissière
and whipped cream**

375g (13¼oz) whole milk

1 egg

3 egg yolks

2 teaspoons vanilla paste

75g (2½oz) caster sugar

30g (1oz) cornflour, sifted

25g (1oz) unsalted butter, cut
into small cubes

125ml (½ cup) double cream

Peter has lots of Norwegian family. When he contacted his cousin Camilla in Horten to ask which cake represents Norway the best, she exclaimed without doubt Kvæfjordkake! Norwegians call it *'verdens beste kake'*, the 'world's best cake.' Cake, meringue and crème pâtissière all on one plate? I think they might be right!

METHOD

Preheat the oven to 160°C fan (350°F) and line a Swiss roll tin with baking parchment.

For the cake, cream the butter and sugar together then slowly whisk in the egg yolks one at a time. Stir in the milk and vanilla then fold in the flour, baking powder and pinch of salt. Spread the cake batter evenly in the tin.

Now make the meringues. Whisk the egg whites with the cream of tartar until soft peaks form. Add the sugar a spoonful at a time until you have a thick, glossy meringue. Spread the meringue mixture on top of the cake mixture, then scatter the flaked almonds on top.

Bake for 35 minutes, or until a skewer comes out clean. Leave to cool for a few minutes in the pan then turn out carefully, so the meringue is still on top.

To make the crème pâtissière, start by heating the milk until nearly boiling.

Put the egg, egg yolks, vanilla, sugar and cornflour in a bowl and whisk together. Slowly pour the hot milk over the egg mixture and whisk together before pouring the mixture back into the pan. Stir over a gentle heat for 1 minute, before bringing to the boil.

Keep stirring until it begins to thicken. Take off the heat and whisk in the cubes of butter until it has combined. Add to a jug, cover in cling film, cool and place the fridge.

To assemble: cut the cake in half, place one half onto a dish and spread a generous layer of crème pâtissière on top. Whip the cream to soft peaks, transfer to a piping bag and pipe on top. Layer the other half of the cake on top and dust with icing sugar.

Place in the fridge for one hour before serving.

SEMLOR

INGREDIENTS

For the buns

425g (15oz) strong white flour

50g (1¾oz) caster sugar

½ teaspoon salt

1 teaspoon cardamom, freshly ground

7g (½oz) instant dried yeast

75g (2½oz) butter, softened

250ml (1 cup) milk

1 egg, lightly beaten

For the glaze

1 egg, lightly beaten

For the filling

200g (7oz) almond paste (I recommend Odense Mandelmassa)

2 tablespoons milk

300ml (1¼ cups) double cream

1 teaspoon caster sugar

½ teaspoon vanilla extract

Icing sugar for dusting

One of Sweden's most beloved seasonal treats are Semla (Semla for singular, Semlor for plural). The day before Lent is celebrated by eating at least one of these! Semla is a bun flavoured with cardamom and filled with almond paste and whipped cream. Bake these and you'll be booking your flights to Stockholm the next day.

METHOD

Add the flour, the sugar, salt and cardamom to a mixing bowl and stir thoroughly, then add the yeast and stir.

Melt the butter in a saucepan and add the milk. Heat until just warm (38°C/100°F). Add the mixture and beaten egg to the flour and stir until you get a sticky dough.

Turn the dough onto a lightly oiled surface and knead for about 10 minutes. Transfer to a bowl, cover with a dish towel and leave to rise in a warm place for about 45 minutes until doubled in size.

Turn the dough onto a lightly floured surface; knead again for 2 to 3 minutes. Divide and shape the dough into 12 balls, then space well on a parchment-lined baking tray. Cover with a damp kitchen towel. Leave to rise for 30 minutes.

Preheat the oven to 180°C fan (400°F).

Lightly glaze the buns with a beaten egg.

Bake the buns in the lower half of the oven for 10 to 12 minutes, until nicely browned. Allow to cool on a wire rack under a kitchen towel.

Once cooled, slice a thin portion off the top of each bun and set aside. Spoon out about a third from the inside of each bun and crumble into a bowl. Grate the almond paste and combine with the crumbs and milk. Blend thoroughly until a thick paste forms. Spoon a generous amount of filling into each hollowed bun.

In a bowl, whip the cream with the sugar and vanilla until soft peaks form. Use a piping bag – fitted with a star nozzle – to pipe into all the buns. Put the lids back on and dust lightly with icing sugar. Serve immediately.

BRØDTORT

SERVES 6

INGREDIENTS

For the cake

150g (5oz) rye bread (even better if it's stale)

150g (5oz) hazelnuts or Brazil nuts

3 tablespoons cocoa powder

1 teaspoon baking powder

6 eggs

200g (7oz) soft dark brown sugar

For the filling and topping

200ml (¾ cup + 1 tablespoon) double cream

100g (3½oz) blackcurrant jam

50g (1¾oz) dark chocolate

Sonderjylland in southern Denmark is famous for its Sønderjysk Kaffebord – a long table topped with everything from sponge cakes, pastries and buns to layer cakes, biscuits and tarts.

No Sønderjysk Kaffebord would be complete without Brødtort. A dense, sour, nutty rye cake sweetened with a filling of cream and jam. For your guests who do not like sweet sponges, they will find this a moreish treat!

METHOD

First, let's make the cake. Preheat the oven to 200°C fan (425°F). Butter and line two 20cm (8") tins.

Blitz the rye bread and the nuts in a food processor to create breadcrumbs. Mix these together with the cocoa powder and baking powder.

Separate your eggs. Whisk the egg yolks and sugar together until light and fluffy. Then fold your dry ingredients into the egg yolk mixture. Whisk the egg whites into stiff peaks, then fold gently into the batter.

Spoon into the prepared tins and bake for 12 minutes or until a skewer comes out clean. Remove from the oven and leave to cool in the tin for 10 minutes before turning out onto a wire rack to cool completely.

Now make the filling and topping: whip the cream until it holds its shape but isn't stiff, and spread half of it on the cake, then top with the blackcurrant jam. Place the second cake gently on top and spread this with the remaining cream.

Hold your chocolate bar with one hand and carefully scrape with a knife to create shavings.

Scatter the chocolate on top of the cake and serve.

KARJALANPIIRAKKA

MAKES 6

INGREDIENTS

For the rice pudding

450ml (1¾ cups +
  1 tablespoon) water

230g (8oz) short-grain rice

450ml (1¾ cups +
  1 tablespoon) milk

2 tablespoons butter

1 teaspoon salt

For the dough

125g (4½oz) rye flour

40g (1½oz) plain flour

120ml (½ cup) water

1 teaspoon salt

To assemble

60ml (¼ cup) milk

50g (1¾oz) butter, melted

3 hard-boiled eggs

4 tablespoons butter,
  softened

Salt and pepper

This pastry from the Karelia region, the eastern part of Finland, proudly has Traditional Speciality Guaranteed status in Europe, just like our Stornoway Black Pudding. The crunch of the rye pastry, the salty rice pudding centre and the buttery egg makes this a delicious breakfast dish. Kiitos Suomi!

METHOD

To make the rice pudding, add the water and the rice to a pan. Bring to the boil, cover and allow to simmer over low heat for 15 minutes. When most of the water is absorbed, add the milk and continue to simmer for about 20 minutes until the rice has a smooth, thick texture. Add the salt and butter, stir and allow to cool completely.

For the dough, first preheat the oven to 240°C fan (500°F) and line a baking tray.

Add the rye and plain flour to a bowl; combine with the salt and water to make a firm dough. Measure out six equal parts and make into balls.

Lightly flour your work surface and roll each ball into an oval shape – about the size of your hand. The thinner the dough, the crispier your rye crust.

To assemble, place 3 tablespoons of the rice filling into the middle of each pie crust.

Crimp the sides of the dough towards the centre, creating waves with your fingers, leaving some of the rice pudding exposed.

Place the pies on a baking tray. Warm the milk, stir in the melted butter and brush onto the crust.

Put in the oven and bake for 6 minutes, then remove and brush with the buttery milk and place immediately back in the oven for another 6 minutes. When golden, remove from the oven, place on a wire rack and brush once more.

Chop up the boiled eggs, mix in the softened butter, season well and top the cooled pies.

HJÓNABANDSSÆLA

SERVES 6

INGREDIENTS

50g (1¾oz) caster sugar

2 tablespoons soft brown sugar

70g (2½oz) rolled oats

125g (4½oz) plain flour

½ teaspoon ground cardamom

1 teaspoon of ground ginger

½ teaspoon of bicarbonate of soda

1 egg

115g (4oz) butter

250g (9oz) rhubarb jam (strawberry or blackcurrant works perfectly too)

The secret to a happy marriage? I think Icelanders have the answer – cake! Hjónabandssæla translates to *blissful marriage cake*. Traditionally it is said that if a wife can make this cake, then the couple will live happily ever after. And seeing Iceland is annually ranked as one of the happiest countries in the world, maybe they're onto something here . . .

METHOD

Add the sugars, oats, flour, cardamom, ginger and bicarbonate of soda into a bowl and mix together.

Use a hand mixer to blend in the egg, then add the butter and make sure all the ingredients are fully combined – but don't overmix.

Wrap the dough and refrigerate for 2 hours.

Preheat oven to 180°C fan (400°F). Grease and line a small cake tin.

Cut about a third of the dough and put aside. Roll out the rest of the dough slightly larger than the tin, press it into the bottom of the tin and a little bit up to the sides. Spread the jam thickly on top.

Now take the rest of the dough, roll it out in thin rolls and lay them across the cake to make a checkerboard pattern.

Bake for 20 to 25 minutes. Rest in the tin for 10 minutes, then place on a wire rack.

LUSIKKALEIVÄT

MAKES 24 BISCUITS

INGREDIENTS

200g (7oz) butter

125g (4½oz) caster sugar + 40g (1½oz) to coat the biscuits

1 teaspoon vanilla extract

300g (10½oz) plain flour

1 teaspoon bicarbonate of soda

75g (2½oz) raspberry jam

The secret to the wonderful flavour of these Finnish Spoon Cookies is the brown butter. Brown butter is melted butter with a nutty flavour brought on by gently cooking it on the stove. These shortbread cookies get their elegant shape from the spoons used to form them. If you can wait, the texture improves the next day and they truly melt in your mouth.

METHOD

Preheat the oven to 175°C fan (385°F) and line a baking sheet.

To brown the butter, melt the butter in a saucepan over a low heat and cook for 10 minutes, stirring regularly. Once it turns golden, pour into a bowl, add the sugar and vanilla, and mix thoroughly. Leave to cool a little, then sieve in the flour and bicarbonate of soda; combine well.

To shape a cookie, press a bit of dough into a large teaspoon, flatten the tops and remove the excess on the sides with a finger. There is enough butter in the dough that the shaped cookie should easily slide out of the spoon.

Place on the baking sheet, flat side down. Bake for 10 to 12 minutes until light golden. Leave to cool completely on a wire rack.

Spread a layer of jam on the flat side of half the biscuits. Sandwich with another biscuit. Finally, add the remaining 40g (1½oz) sugar to a bowl and roll each biscuit in the sugar until coated.

KRONANS KAKA

INGREDIENTS

150g (5oz) potatoes

75g (2½oz) butter

75g (2½oz) caster sugar

2 eggs

1 teaspoon almond extract

100g (3½oz) ground almonds

1 teaspoon baking powder

20g (¾oz) flaked almonds

Icing sugar, to dust

Kronans Kaka means *The Crown's Cake*. Kronan, the Crown, is an old Swedish name for the army and this cake was served to soldiers for over a century. It was an economical dish as it was baked without flour (which was scarce at the time) and used leftover potato. Though an uncommon ingredient, the potato gives the cake a creamy texture which compliments the wonderful almondy flavour. It is the perfect bake for people looking for a gluten-free treat.

METHOD

Peel and chop your potatoes then boil until cooked. Drain and, once cooled, mash together.

Preheat oven to 180°C fan (400°F). Grease and line a 20cm (8") cake tin.

Cream the butter and sugar together, then mix in the eggs one at a time along with the almond extract. Mix in the ground almonds and baking powder. Finally add the mashed potato, making sure it is well blended into the batter.

Bake for 20 minutes or until a skewer comes out clean. Cool on a wire rack. When serving, dust with icing sugar, then toast some flaked almonds in a pan and scatter over the top.

KÄRLEKSMUMS

MAKES 12 SQUARES

INGREDIENTS

For the cake

50ml (3 tablespoons +
  1 teaspoon) water

3½ tablespoons cocoa
  powder

150ml (½ cup +
  2 tablespoons) milk

200g (7oz) butter

225g (8oz) caster sugar

3 eggs

1 teaspoon vanilla extract

225g (8oz) plain flour

1 teaspoon bicarbonate of
  soda

For the topping

60g (2oz) butter

4 tablespoons instant coffee

1 tablespoon cocoa powder

150g (5oz) icing sugar

75g (2½oz) desiccated
  coconut

When you find a cake whose name translates as *love yums*, you know it's going to be good. And in the best possible way, this reminds me of a tray bake you would find at a church fête or school social. This wonderful cake is light and fluffy, which goes perfectly with the coffee-infused chocolatey topping and the signature coconut sprinkling.

METHOD

Preheat the oven to 160°C fan (350°F), then grease and line a 20cm (8″) square tin.

Boil the water and stir in the cocoa powder. Once cooled, stir in the milk.

Into a bowl add your butter and sugar and whisk together before adding in one egg at a time along with the vanilla extract until combined.

Sift in your flour and bicarbonate of soda, then pour in your cocoa milk mixture and whisk until just combined.

Add to your prepared tin and bake for 20 to 25 minutes until a skewer comes out clean. Leave in the tin for 5 minutes then cool on a wire rack.

To make the topping add the butter, coffee, cocoa and icing sugar into a pan over a low heat until the butter has melted. Stir in 50g (1¾oz) of the coconut and spread over the cake. Sprinkle the extra coconut and leave to set. Don't wait for a church fête to serve!

A GAELIC SONG FOR EUROPE

'Thank goodness for Engelbert Humperdinck,' I said as our bus trundled down the motorway from Gardermoen Airport in Oslo. Sitting beside me was Joy Dunlop. 'Thank goodness for Engelbert Humperdinck!' she repeated, chuckling as we reminisced about a message I had sent her seven years previously . . .

It all began on the night of the Eurovision Song Contest 2012. As Loreen reprised the winning entry for Sweden, the scoreboard showed the United Kingdom second bottom of the scoreboard. Engelbert's slow waltz had not wowed the judges, or me. Meanwhile I was texting Joy: 'Let's enter a Gaelic song for Eurovision!' The reply was immediate: 'That is my dream, let's do it!' The messages went back and forth with emojis of musical notes, Scotland flags, fireworks and smiley faces. And that night, the die was cast.

Joy is a renowned Gaelic singer, TV presenter, Royal National Mòd Gold Medallist and damn fine cèilidh dancer (I can tell you that from first-hand experience!) And okay, it took us some time, but seven years later that bus was taking us to Gothenburg, Sweden to perform with Alba, a Gaelic choir who were the Scotland entry at the 2019 Eurovision Choir Song Contest.

Nine months earlier in a Glasgow café, I sat across from Margaret Cameron, the BBC Alba Commissioner, and presented my idea of a Gaelic choir representing Scotland at Eurovision. If she thought I was mad, she hid it well. She listened intently to my plan of how a Gaelic song could be heard by millions across Europe. She took a sip from her cup, looked up and said, 'Let's do it.' I'm not sure of the etiquette of hugging BBC commissioners, but I jumped up, threw my arms around her, then ran out the door before she changed her mind!

Choral music has been an integral part of Gaelic musical culture for over a century. The pinnacle is performing at the Lovat & Tullibardine competition at the annual Royal National Mòd, which was first won by Dundee Gaelic Choir in 1903. Each choir is required to perform two songs in front of a set of judges who will decide the winner.

I had sung tenor in the Glasgow Islay Gaelic Choir since 2003 and performed at the Lovat & Tullibardine competition fourteen times, learning everything from the inspirational conductor Kirsteen Grant. As a Mòd Gold Medallist herself, she knew what it took to create a performance and the choir was filled with amazing vocalists, some of who had sung in the choir for over fifty years. It was choir members Irene and Fiona that encouraged Peter and I to sing together at the Mòd. They had competed as a duet at the Mòd for many years and won

the competition a remarkable eight times. Their encouragement and Kirsteen's musical arrangement of the Cape Breton tune 'Tàladh na Beinne Guirme' were the reason we took the winning prize in 2018.

At Alba's first rehearsal, Joy handed out the sheet music of the three tunes we would perform at the contest. The lament 'Cumha na Cloinne' is a *pìobaireachd*, a piece of bagpipe music, composed by Pàdraig Mòr MacCrimmon in 1650 after the death of seven of his children. This stirring composition was complemented by intertwining the rhythmic waulking song 'Ach a'Mhairead' – where the woman talks of unrequited love and telling that no kind of music will lift her spirits – with one of the most iconic modern Gaelic rock songs of our era 'Alba' by Runrig.

We were only three lines into the lament and I could feel myself choking up and the tears running down my cheeks. I looked at Joy, who was conducting the choir, and I could see it was having the same effect on her. I don't know if it was Sileas Sinclair's beautiful arrangement of the song or the reality that our dream of entering Eurovision was coming true. Either way, being with a choir made up of Gaelic singers from across the country was already turning into an amazing adventure.

The weeks went by and rehearsals were in full swing. The songs were fine tuned, the choreography was finding its step and the BBC Alba cameras began following us for a documentary that would be shown the night before the live contest. Soon, Joy and I were boarding a flight to Israel – we were invited to attend the 64th Eurovision Song Contest in Tel-Aviv to announce Scotland's debut at Eurovision Choir. As we arrived into the arena, the Norwegian band Keiino had just walked in to their press conference. On the flight over, Joy and I both agreed this was our favourite song in the contest and, for fun, began translating their upbeat pop song 'Spirit in the Sky', which included lyrics in Sámi, into Gaelic. When we told them we were going to be performing our song in Gaelic at the contest, Fred, one of their singers exclaimed, 'I studied Gaelic at Sabhal Mòr Ostaig!'

Sabhal Mòr Ostaig is the National Centre for Gaelic, based in Sleat on the Isle of Skye. It has short courses and degrees in language, culture, teacher training, traditional music and Celtic studies.

Fred grew up in Sámi Norway and his passion for indigenous languages inspired him to visit and learn more about our language. We told him we had learned their song in Gaelic and excitedly he said, 'Let's sing together!' Ten minutes later, we were performing their song live on Norwegian TV in Gaelic and Sámi. Our goal to promote the Gaelic language and music on the European stage had begun!

As the bus arrived at the Partille Arena in Gothenburg, the stage was set for our first rehearsal. We all took an intake of breath as we walked onto the massive stage for the first time. We got word from home that there had been an announcement in the Scottish parliament that day wishing us luck, and we even got a personal message from the First Minister, Nicola Sturgeon. The outpouring of support from all our friends and family was amazing and everyone we knew was planning to be in front of their televisions that night – we felt honoured to represent the Gaelic community and Scotland.

Four singers from each choir were asked to perform the opening of the show. As Nicola, Ainsley, Alasdair and I stood on the darkened stage waiting for the iconic Eurovision music to begin, I squeezed Nicola's hand beside me. If only my ten-year-old self could see me now, about to sing ABBA's hit 'Mamma Mia' live on television across Europe.

We would perform seventh on the night along with the other choirs representing Sweden, Belgium, Latvia, Germany, Norway, Denmark, Slovenia, Switzerland and Wales. When it was our turn to perform, there was time for a final hug with Joy backstage – we had been on the most unbelievable adventure and at the centre of it was being able to promote our language, culture and music.

We sang our hearts out – it was the best we have ever performed. And when Denmark was announced the winner, I don't think any of us felt anything but proud. I will never forget the scenes after the show when we sang our song outside the arena surrounded by all the other choirs cheering us along.

Not since 1966 and Kenneth McKellar had Eurovision seen a kilt on stage. I hope it will return.

In the words of ABBA: *Taing dhuibh airson a'chiùil* – Thank you for the music.

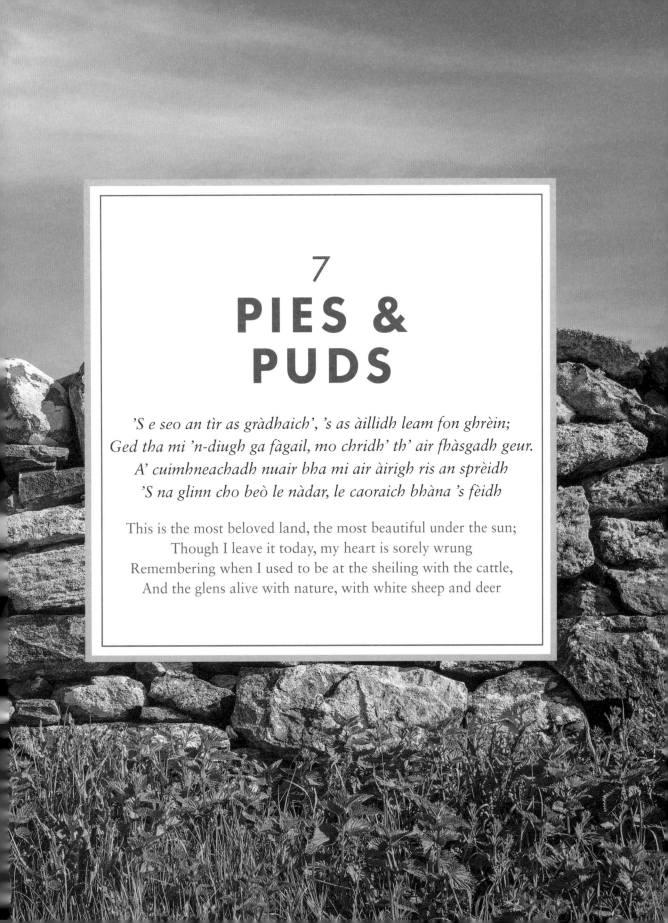

7
PIES & PUDS

'S e seo an tìr as gràdhaich', 's as àillidh leam fon ghrèin;
Ged tha mi 'n-diugh ga fàgail, mo chridh' th' air fhàsgadh geur.
A' cuimhneachadh nuair bha mi air àirigh ris an sprèidh
'S na glinn cho beò le nàdar, le caoraich bhàna 's fèidh

This is the most beloved land, the most beautiful under the sun;
Though I leave it today, my heart is sorely wrung
Remembering when I used to be at the sheiling with the cattle,
And the glens alive with nature, with white sheep and deer

JOY'S SALTED CARAMEL & TABLET CHEESECAKE

SERVES 8

INGREDIENTS

For the tablet

450g (1lb) granulated sugar

250ml (1 cup) milk

1 tablespoon golden syrup

60g (2oz) butter

1 teaspoon vanilla essence

For the salted caramel

75g (2½oz) butter

100g (3½oz) soft light brown sugar

50g (1¾oz) golden syrup

125ml (½ cup) double cream

½ teaspoon sea salt

For the cheesecake

75g (2½oz) butter

250g (9oz) digestive biscuits

600g (1lb 5oz) cream cheese

75g (2½oz) icing sugar

1 teaspoon vanilla extract

250ml (1 cup) double cream

There's only one person in the world that has a sweeter tooth than me and that's Joy! Her cheesecake is swirled and topped with perfectly-made vanilla tablet along with a salted caramel sauce for extra indulgence.

METHOD

In a pan over gentle heat, warm the sugar, milk and golden syrup. Stir occasionally until the sugar is dissolved, then add the butter and melt.

Bring the mix slowly to boiling point. Now increase the heat and stir continuously until the mixture has reached soft-ball stage at 120°C (248°F).

Take off the heat and add the vanilla essence. Beat until almost setting in the pan. Pour into a well-greased baking tin with a low lip and allow to set.

After 30 minutes, score into wee bite-sized pieces, then once it has completely cooled cut into pieces.

For the salted caramel, melt the butter, sugar and golden syrup in a pan. Simmer for 3 minutes, stirring every now and again. Add the cream and sea salt; simmer for another minute, then pour into a jug for serving.

To make the cheesecake, melt the butter in a pan. Crush the digestives into crumbs, tip into the melted butter and stir to combine.

Take a 18cm (7") springform tin. Tip in the biscuit mix and press down, using the back of a spoon to smooth it. Chill in the fridge for an hour.

Beat the cream cheese, icing sugar and vanilla together briefly. Add the double cream one third at a time, allowing the mixture to thicken before adding more. Dice 150g (5oz) of the tablet into wee cubes and stir into the mixture. Top the biscuit base with the cream cheese mixture and smooth out. Chill in the fridge overnight.

Pour a layer of the salted caramel sauce on top of the cheesecake (serve the remaining sauce in a jug). Finally, chop another 150g (5oz) of tablet into crumbs and sprinkle on top.

PLUM & APPLE GALETTE

SERVES 4

INGREDIENTS

For the pastry

80g (2¾oz) hazelnuts

2 tablespoons icing sugar

125g (4½oz) spelt flour, plus extra for dusting

175g (6¼oz) plain flour

150g (5oz) cold butter, cubed

Pinch of salt

1–2 tablespoons water

1 egg, beaten

For the fruit filling

3 plums, stones removed and chopped

2 Bramley apples, cored and sliced

50g (1¾oz) light brown soft sugar

½ lemon, zested and juiced

1 tablespoon cornflour

1 tablespoon golden syrup

This rustic-looking, golden, French, filled tart is the perfect bake to house autumnal fruits. With the edges roughly folded in to create a gorgeous, free-form pie, it is delicious served warm from the oven with cream or ice cream.

METHOD

To make the pastry, add the hazelnuts and icing sugar in a food processor and blitz together. Add the spelt and plain flour, butter and a pinch of salt, and blitz again until combined; if needed add in a tablespoon of water at a time until the dough starts to form in clumps. On your work surface, knead briefly and shape into a disc, then wrap and chill for 30 minutes.

In a bowl, toss the sliced plums and apples in a mix of the brown sugar, lemon zest, cornflour and golden syrup and leave aside.

Preheat the oven to 160°C fan (350°F).

Sprinkle spelt flour on baking parchment that will line your baking tray. Roll out the pastry to a 30–35cm (12–14") circle – don't worry if it looks rustic. Place onto the baking tray and scatter the sliced plums and apples in the middle of the pastry, leaving a thick border around the edges. Fold the overhanging pasty, using the baking parchment to help you lift the edges of the pastry over the fruit, but leaving most of the fruit exposed.

Brush the edges with the beaten egg, and sprinkle with a little extra brown sugar. Bake for 45 minutes.

Meanwhile, pour any leftover syrup from the fruit into a saucepan, simmer until syrupy and when the galette comes out of the oven, brush over the top of the fruit.

Leave to cool slightly and then serve.

TREACLE TOFFEE BANOFFEE

SERVES 6

INGREDIENTS

For the base

250g (9oz) digestive biscuits

1 teaspoon mixed spice

100g (3½oz) butter, melted

For the filling

100g (3½oz) butter

50g (1¾oz) caster sugar

50g (1¾oz) soft dark brown sugar

400g (14oz) can condensed milk

1 tablespoon black treacle

For the topping

4 bananas

300ml (1¼ cups) double cream

2 tablespoons soft brown sugar

1 tablespoon butter

50g (1¾oz) dark chocolate

Everyone needs a few easy no-bake desserts in their collection and Banoffee Pie is a firm family favourite. It's as much about the textures as it is the flavour. It is creamy, soft, chewy and crumbly all at the same time.

I never thought you could improve on a classic Banoffee Pie recipe until I added a tablespoon of black treacle to the filling and a hint of mixed spice to the digestive base. Perfect for a special treat or a Sunday gathering (stretchy pants optional!).

METHOD

To make the base, put the digestive biscuits in a sealable food bag and bash with a rolling pin. Tip into a bowl, add in the mixed spice and stir in the melted butter.

Press the mixture into the base and part way up the sides of a 20cm (8") spring-form cake tin, then place in the fridge to chill for 30 minutes.

Now make the filling. Add the butter and both types of sugar in a saucepan over a low heat, stirring until the butter has melted and the sugars dissolve. Add the condensed milk and bring gently to the boil, stirring continuously to make a golden caramel. As soon as it comes to the boil, remove from the heat, then stir in the black treacle.

Spread the filling over the biscuit base and chill for about an hour.

About 15 minutes before you are going to remove the pie from the fridge, slice three of the bananas and place a layer over the treacle toffee. Whip your cream into soft peaks and spoon over the bananas.

To decorate, slice the remaining banana down the middle. In a large frying pan, heat the sugar over a moderate heat and then stir in the butter. Add the banana cut-side down and return to the heat; cook for 2 minutes and then turn over, and the banana should take on a caramel colour. Place on top of the pie and scatter with chocolate shavings.

PEAR & APPLE SPONGE

SERVES 6

INGREDIENTS

For the fruit layer

2 (about 500g/1lb 2oz) Bramley apples

3–4 (500g/1lb 2oz) pears

½ lemon, juiced

80g (2¾oz) caster sugar

For the sponge

115g (4oz) butter

115g (4oz) caster sugar, plus extra for sprinkling

100g (3½oz) self-raising flour

75g (2½oz) ground almonds

3 eggs, beaten

½ teaspoon almond extract

If I had to choose one recipe in the book that literally is a hug on a plate, this is it. The golden, almondy sponge tops perfectly baked apples and pears. It is so simple to make and your guests will definitely be asking for seconds – lucky this is a family-sized pudding!

METHOD

Preheat the oven to 160°C fan (350°F).

Start by preparing the fruits. Chop the apples and pears into similar-sized chunks and put into a bowl with the lemon juice. Add the sugar, mix thoroughly, then tip into a 1.5-litre (1.5-quart) pie dish.

Next, make the sponge. In a bowl, cream the butter and sugar together until light and fluffy. In another bowl, mix together the flour and almonds. Whisk a third of the eggs into the butter, then a third of the flour mixture and repeat until you've used up the ingredients. Stir in the almond extract and layer over the fruit. Bake for 50 minutes or until the topping has risen into a golden sponge. Sprinkle with extra sugar and serve warm with a large jug of custard at the ready!

SWEET 'SHIRE PUDDINGS WITH CUSTARD & JAM

MAKES 6

INGREDIENTS

For the puddings

150g (5oz) plain flour

¼ teaspoon sea salt

2 eggs

100ml (⅓ cup +
    1 tablespoon) cold water

150ml (½ cup +
    2 tablespoons) milk

½ orange, zested

½ teaspoon vanilla extract

50ml (3 tablespoons +
    1 teaspoon) sunflower oil

For the homemade
custard

1 vanilla pod

50g (1¾oz) sugar

2 egg yolks

1 teaspoon cornflour

150ml (½ cup +
    2 tablespoons) double
    cream

150ml (½ cup +
    2 tablespoons) milk

To assemble

Your favourite jam (mine's
    raspberry)

Nothing beats Yorkshire Puddings filled with gravy served with your roast dinner, but how's about adding a twist to these puds for dessert? Add orange zest and vanilla to the batter for a sweet treat!

METHOD

Prepare the batter in the morning or at least an hour before you plan to serve them. Add the flour and salt to a jug, then crack in the eggs.

Combine the water and milk, then whisk into the batter. Stir in the orange zest and vanilla extract. Rest the batter in the fridge.

When ready to cook, preheat the oven to 220°C fan (465°F). Divide the oil between the holes of a muffin tin and place in the oven to heat up for 7 minutes. Once hot, remove the tin from the oven and evenly pour the batter into the hot oil in each of the holes.

Immediately return the tin to the oven and cook for 15 to 17 minutes until they are golden and puffed up. Just don't be tempted to open the oven door too early! Meanwhile, to make the custard, slice the vanilla pod and scrape out the vanilla seeds.

In a bowl, whisk together your sugar and egg yolks until shiny and pale. Add cornflour and whisk again.

Into a saucepan, add your cream, milk and vanilla seeds as well as the pod. Simmer but take off the heat before it boils and remove the vanilla pod. Whisking constantly, pour a wee bit of the hot milk over the egg mixture. Keep adding a wee bit at a time and stir until it is all combined. Place this back on a low heat, stirring constantly for 5 to 7 minutes.

You know it's ready when you can draw a clear line through the custard on the back of a spoon. You want it thick but still pourable.

To assemble, place a pudding (or two!) into a bowl, fill with a tablespoon of your favourite jam and then smother with custard.

PWDIN MYNWY

INGREDIENTS

For the custard

600ml (2⅓ cups) milk

25g (1oz) butter, plus extra
for greasing the dish

1 lemon, zested

50g (1¾oz) caster sugar

3 eggs yolks (keep the whites
for the meringue)

75g (2½oz) fresh white
breadcrumbs

120g (4oz) raspberry jam

For the meringue

175g (6¼oz) caster sugar

3 egg whites

Na Dùthchannan Ceilteach is the Gaelic name for the Celtic nations, made up of Breizh (Brittany), Kernow (Cornwall), Éire (Ireland), Ellan Vannin (Isle of Man), Alba (Scotland) and Cymru (Wales). Pwdin Mynwy is a traditional Welsh pudding from Monmouth which bakes breadcrumbs in a custard, topped with jam and toasted meringue. As they say in Welsh, blasus!

METHOD

Preheat the oven to 150°C fan (340°F) and grease a 1.4-litre (1.4-quart) dish with butter.

Warm the milk in a saucepan. Stir in the butter, lemon zest and sugar until dissolved.

Meanwhile, whisk the yolks into a large bowl. Then a bit at a time, slowly pour the warm milk into the yolks, and continue to whisk.

Add the breadcrumbs to the buttered dish and pour over the custardy mixture. Leave to rest for about 15 minutes. The breadcrumbs will soak up the custard.

Place the dish in a roasting tin and fill the tin halfway with hot water. Bake for 25 minutes until the custard has set. Remove from the oven and set aside to cool a little.

Meanwhile, make the meringue. Whisk the egg whites until stiff peaks form, then a tablespoon at a time add the sugar while continuing to whisk. You should have a thick and shiny meringue.

Lower the oven temperature to 130°C fan (300°F).

Spread a layer of raspberry jam over the set custard, then add the meringue to a piping bag and pipe on top.

Bake in the oven for about 15 minutes until the meringue is toasted on top and serve immediately.

SPICED PLUM CRUMBLE

SERVES 6

INGREDIENTS

For the spiced plums

12 plums, cut in half and
    stones removed

50g (1¾oz) butter

150g (5oz) blackberries

1 vanilla pod, split

2 cinnamon sticks

100ml (⅓ cup +
    1 tablespoon) red wine

5 tablespoons golden syrup

4 tablespoons caster sugar

For the topping

50g (1¾oz) amaretti biscuits

150g (5oz) rolled oats

70g (2½oz) plain flour

125g (4½oz) soft brown
    sugar

175g (6¼oz) butter, melted

2 tablespoons golden syrup

Crumble originates from Second World War rationing, when you couldn't always count on having enough ingredients to make a full pie, but nowadays they are a culinary celebration and I couldn't imagine a chapter of puddings and pies without one! This recipe's sticky-sweet plums are complimented with the oaty amaretti topping, for this perfect late-autumn dish. Oh and while you're on the islands, this Gaelic phrase might come in handy: 'Steallag eile de dh' ughagan, mas e do thoil e!' – it means 'another spoonful of custard, please'!

METHOD

Preheat the oven to 180°C fan (400°F).

Sauté the halved plums with the butter in a frying pan for a few minutes. Add the blackberries, split vanilla pod, cinnamon sticks, red wine, golden syrup and sugar, then bring to the boil and simmer gently for 8 minutes, allowing the sauce to thicken. Place in an ovenproof dish.

In another bowl, crush the amaretti biscuits (not into crumbs but different sized pieces). Add your oats, flour, sugar and then stir in your melted butter and golden syrup.

Coat the plums in the crumble and bake in the oven for 20 to 25 minutes or until golden brown.

Remove from the oven and allow to cool slightly before serving with vanilla custard.

BAKED OAT ALASKA

For the honey, oat and raspberry sponge

75g (2½oz) butter

60g (2oz) soft brown sugar

½ teaspoon vanilla essence

25g (1oz) honey

1 egg

30g (1oz) oats

80g (2¾oz) self-raising flour

60g (2oz) raspberries

For the vanilla oat ice cream

75g (2½oz) pinhead oatmeal

200g (7oz) granulated sugar

60g (2oz) water

500g (1lb 2oz) vanilla ice cream

For the meringue

4 egg whites

175g (6¼oz) caster sugar

Pinch of cream of tartar

Did you know there was a World Porridge Making Championship? The hotly contested Golden Spurtle is awarded in Carrbridge, Scotland annually. The 2021 tournament went online and I entered with my Baked Oat Alaska, putting an oaty twist on this retro dessert. Though I was pipped at the post and finished in second place, I was very proud of my entry!

METHOD

For the honey, oat and raspberry sponge

Preheat the oven to 160°C (350°F) then grease and line a 15cm (6") cake tin.

Cream the butter, sugar, vanilla and honey until light and fluffy. Then beat in the egg.

Blitz the oats in a food processor until they have the consistency of flour.

Fold the flour and oats into the wet mixture, then finally stir in the raspberries.

Pour into the cake tin and bake for 20 to 25 minutes or until a skewer comes out clean. Place on a wire rack to cool.

For the vanilla oat ice cream

Toast your pinhead oats in a frying pan and set aside.

In a saucepan stir the granulated sugar and water together over moderate heat until all the sugar granules have dissolved completely, then boil for about 4 minutes until it begins to turn a caramel colour. Swirl the syrup in the pan every 20 seconds. Quickly, take off the heat and stir in the toasted pinhead oats into the syrup and immediately pour onto baking parchment. When set, bash with a spurtle into wee pieces.

Take the vanilla ice cream out of the freezer to soften.

Line a Pyrex bowl (a similar size to your cake tin) with cling film, spoon in the softened vanilla ice cream and stir in the crushed pieces of pinhead caramel. Place this in the freezer for at least 1 hour to set.

(continues overleaf)

For the meringue

Whisk your egg whites to soft peaks, add your cream of tartar and whisk again. A spoonful at a time, whisk in your sugar. It should appear thick and shiny when done.

To assemble

Pre-heat your oven to 180°C fan (400°F).

Put your oat sponge on a baking tray lined with baking parchment. Remove the ice cream from the cling film and place it on top of the sponge.

Using a spatula, cover with the meringue, ensuring that the ice cream and sponge are completely covered with no gaps. Smooth the meringue into swirled peaks.

Bake for 5 minutes, until lightly golden. Serve immediately.

UNDER THE ROWAN TREE

When you visit the Outer Hebrides, you'll be welcomed by sweeping sandy beaches, epic landscapes, heather-topped mountains and a myriad of lochs, but on your travels around the islands, you might notice there is one thing missing – trees.

Some claim the Vikings stripped the island of trees to prevent rivals from using the wood to build boats; others believe that severe storms about 8000 years ago felled the trees and left the landscape dominated by moorland. These long, vast stretches of moorland are where we go to cut the peats for our winter fires with a tool left by Norsemen called a *tarsgeir*. It has a long wooden handle with an angled blade on the end that both cuts and turns the peat. Ask any expat Hebridean to name something that reminds them of home, and the smell of peat is likely to be near the top of the list!

Usually after the *sealastair* or yellow iris has flowered in May, the men and women of the villages would head to the moor, with each croft allotted its own peat bank. Stacking the dried peats in a tidy fashion beside your house in a *cruach-mòine* is like an Olympic sport and my mother would have been a gold medalist. Folk used to come to visit my mother just to see hers being built. The design of a finished *cruach*, as a peat-stack is known in Gaelic, is both functional (to keep the peat dry) and a work of art, delicately intertwining herring bone patterns to the end of the *cruach* – just like you can see in home-woven Harris Tweed patterns. The moors are covered in wild heather and their contrast to the open skies is breathtaking. But rarely are there any trees growing on these exposed, windy stretches.

Growing up, we had two rowan trees on our croft. They were very useful for sheltering under in the rain but, most importantly, for their berries to make jam, as their fruit naturally contains pectin which sets jams perfectly. The rowan tree has a long, sacred history. Since ancient times people have been planting a rowan beside their home as in Celtic mythology it symbolises courage, wisdom and protection, especially from evil spirits and misfortune. The rowan also features in Norse mythology and legend has it that it saved the life of the god Thor by bending over a fast-flowing river in the Underworld in which he was being swept away. Thor managed to grab the tree and get back to the shore.

Nature is at the heart of the Gaelic language, and even if you don't speak it, you might be using Gaelic words every day without knowing it. Travelling through its towns, villages, mountains and lochs, the language has left its imprint on so much of Scotland.

Like *baile* (village), as in Ballachulish, *druim* (ridge) in Drumnadrochit and *inbhir* (mouth of the river) as in Inverness, Invergordon or Inveraray.

When Pàdruig, Seòras and I travel across the Minch by ferry from the Isle of Harris, we always stop for a cuppa and cake in the village of Portree, the capital of the Isle of Skye. Its name comes from the Gaelic *Port Rìgh* and translates as the King's Port, possibly from a visit by King James V of Scotland in 1540. And as we drive south past the many Munros (the name for the 282 Scottish mountains over 3,000 feet in height) they feature Gaelic words like *beinn* (mountain), *creag* (rock/cliff) and mullach (summit). Suppose you're heading up for a day on the *Aonach Eagach* (jagged ridge) north of Glencoe. Your first climb takes you to *Am Bodach* (the old man) while to your east, you might spy his counterpart, *A' Chailleach* (the old woman)!

If you've watched BBC Alba over the past couple of years, you'll have seen Pàdruig and Seòras popping up on your screens on their TV show *Gàrradh Phàdruig* – Peter's Garden. I've been lucky enough to benefit from the bountiful fruits and vegetables that he's grown, though his real passion is Scotland's native woodlands. On our journeys between Oban and Lewis he is always pointing out a Scots pine, oak or silver birch. Much of the Highlands and what is now the Cairngorms National Park was once covered with the Caledonian Forest. The Scots pine trees found here are directly descended from the native pinewoods that grew around 7,000 BC. Beneath the vast forest canopy, the likes of wild boar, lynx, brown bears and grey wolves – all now extinct in the wild in Scotland – roamed. But the Caledonian Forest is still home to some of the rarest wildlife in the Scotland, including mountain hare, pine marten, red squirrel, wildcats and capercaillie.

The Gaelic alphabet itself holds a respect for nature. We have only eighteen letters in our alphabet and all of them co-exist in the English alphabet, but we lack the j, k, q, v, w, x, y, z, making Gaelic a very low-scoring language to play Scrabble in! Each letter is represented by a tree or plant name, allowing the language to intertwine with the mythology and stories behind them.

The first letter in the alphabet is Ailm. In folklore, elm trees were long associated with the Underworld. It was said the trees had a special affinity with elves who guarded the burial mounds and their dead. The most common species in Scotland is the wych elm, known in Gaelic as *leamhan*. Norse mythology also claims that the first humans called Ask (ash tree in Norwegian) and Embla (elm tree in Norwegian) were fashioned from tree trunks.

B is for Beith. The silver birch is one of the most sacred trees in Celtic mythology, symbolising new beginnings and protection. The tree was thought to carry ancient wisdom and yet appeared forever young. I wonder if this is why, when you go to a sauna in Scandinavia, they beat birch branches against your skin to stimulate your circulation?

C is for Coll, the word associated with hazel. In modern Gaelic we say *calltainn*. The legend tells us that there were nine hazel trees that grew around a sacred pool, and as the hazelnuts began to drop and flow into the streams, the salmon ate the nuts and became wise. In a story from Irish mythology the Salmon of Knowledge was caught by the poet Finegas and eaten by Fionn mac Cumhaill. It is still common to find hazel trees by wells near abbeys and churches around the country.

But Pàdruig's favourite tree is represented by the letter Iogh which denotes the yew tree. Yew's Gaelic name is *iubhair* and it came to symbolise death and resurrection in Celtic

culture as the ageing branches of yew trees can root and form new trunks where they touch the ground. Its poisonous needles even inspired Macbeth to concoct a deadly drink which included *slips of yew, silvered in the moon's eclipse*. I'd better be careful the next time he makes me a cup of tea!

So, although you won't come across too many trees on the islands, there are of course a few exceptions. Visitors to Stornoway can visit Lews Castle, home to Museum nan Eilean where you can see some of the mysterious Lewis Chessmen which were found in sand dunes in Ardoil, Uig. The woods in the grounds surrounding the castle are remarkable; their planting was a passion project for Lady Matheson, whose husband built the castle in 1863.

The two rowan trees in the croft still stand proudly today – and no doubt will be used to make plenty jars of jam for years to come.

8
NOLLAIG CHRIDHEIL

*Dèan cnuasachd 's an
t-Samhradh, a nì an Geamhradh
a chur seachad.*

Gather in summer what you'll put by for the winter

MULLED PEAR & PISTACHIO PAVLOVA

SERVES 6

INGREDIENTS

For the meringue

6 egg whites

350g (12½oz) caster sugar

1½ teaspoons cornflour

1½ teaspoons white wine or cider vinegar

40g (1½oz) pistachios

For the mulled pears

1 bottle (75cl) red wine

500ml (2 cups) water

1 orange, pared, zested and juiced

1 lemon, pared and zested

5 cloves

2 cinnamon sticks

125g (4½oz) caster sugar

6 pears (Bosc pears are a perfect choice), peeled and with stalks on

150g (5oz) blackberries

400ml (1⅔ cups) double cream

25g (1oz) pistachios, crushed

This is a showstopper dessert and a recipe I return to every Christmas. The meringue will be crispy on the outside, soft and mallowy on the inside, and it contrasts perfectly with the tartness of the pears, the billowy cream and the crushed pistachios. You can make the meringue and pears in advance, but make sure you prepare the cream just when you are going to construct and serve the pavlova.

METHOD

Let's make the meringues first. Preheat the oven to 120°C fan (248°F). Draw a 20cm (8") circle on a sheet of baking parchment.

In a bowl, whisk the egg whites until they form stiff peaks. Add the sugar a spoonful at a time, whisking until you have a stiff and glossy meringue. Then, whisk in the cornflour and vinegar until combined. Swirl the pistachios through your meringue.

Carefully spoon the meringue onto the circle on the baking parchment, and use a palette knife to flatten to top.

Bake for 1 hour, then turn the oven off and leave the meringue inside for at least 2 hours to dry out as it cools.

Now for the mulled pears. Pour the wine and water into a pan. Add all the other ingredients, except the pears and blackberries, put over a low heat and stir until the sugar has dissolved. Bring to the boil and simmer for 5 minutes. Remove from the heat and leave to infuse for 20 minutes.

Return the pan to the heat, adding the pears and blackberries. Bring to a simmer and submerge the pears for 45 minutes. Turn them every 10 minutes. They should be ruby red and just cooked. Remove from the pan and set aside to cool.

Sieve the poaching liquid. Bring back to the boil, reduce until thick and syrupy, then cool.

Place your meringue on a plate. Whip the double cream until soft peaks form and layer over the meringue. Stand the pears on top of the cream in a circle, pour the syrup over and let it drizzle down the sides of the meringue. Finally, sprinkle the pistachios over the top. Serve immediately.

CHRISTMAS EVE CHRISTMAS CAKE

INGREDIENTS

For the cake

150ml (½ cup + 2 table-
 spoons) whisky or brandy

150g (5oz) stem ginger,
 plus 100ml (⅓ cup +
 1 tablespoon) ginger syrup
 from the jar

150g (5oz) raisins

200g (7oz) sultanas

200g (7oz) currants

50g (1¾oz) dried mixed peel

100g (3½oz) glacé cherries

2 tablespoons marmalade

300g (10½oz) plain flour

2 teaspoons baking powder

2 teaspoons mixed spice

200g (7oz) softened butter

200g (7oz) soft light brown
 sugar

4 eggs

2 tablespoons milk

2 oranges, finely zested

2 lemons, finely zested

50g (1¾oz) ground almonds

To decorate

3 tablespoons marmalade

300g (10½oz) marzipan

300g (10½oz) icing

1 teaspoon whisky, brandy
 or rum

Icing sugar, for dusting

Cinnamon sticks, holly leaves
 and a ribbon

Traditionally you would start making your Christmas Cake before Halloween, allowing it to mature by feeding it with a dram of whisky every week. This ginger and marmalade Christmas cake can be made last minute – and your guests will never know! This rustic decoration with cinnamon sticks, holly and a Christmas tree bauble brings a lovely homemade look to the bake.

METHOD

Gently warm the whisky in a saucepan. Chop up the stem ginger and place along with the raisins, sultanas, currants, mixed peel and cherries in a bowl. Pour over the warmed alcohol and stir in the ginger syrup and marmalade. Set aside for 30 minutes.

Preheat the oven to 140°C fan (325°F). Grease and line a 20cm (8") cake tin.

Sift the flour, baking powder and mixed spice into a bowl then add along all the rest of the ingredients. Whisk together until blended together and pale. Fold in the soaked dried fruits and any liquid left in the bowl.

Pour the batter into the cake tin and bake for 1½ to 1¾ hours (cover loosely with foil after an hour if it's getting too dark) until golden brown and a skewer comes out clean. Leave to rest for 10 minutes before placing on a wire rack.

Once cooled you can decorate. Sit the cake on a cake stand, warm the marmalade in a pan and brush a layer of marmalade over the cake.

Dust the work surface with icing sugar. Lightly knead the marzipan, then roll out into a circular shape, large enough to cover the top of the cake, and lift onto the cake. Repeat the process with the icing, but before you place onto the cake, brush the marzipan with a teaspoon of whisky.

To decorate, tie a ribbon loosely around the cake and then begin to place the cinnamon sticks rustically around the cake. Top with holly leaves and your favourite Christmas decoration before setting in the middle of your festive table.

BODACH NA NOLLAIG

MAKES 12

INGREDIENTS

For the chocolate brownie

225g (8oz) butter

450g (16oz) caster sugar

140g (5oz) dark chocolate, broken into pieces

5 eggs

110g (4oz) plain flour

55g (6oz) cocoa powder

For the meringues

2 egg whites

200g (7oz) white caster sugar

40ml (2 tablespoons + 2 teaspoons) red food colouring paste

For the frosting

25g (1oz) soft butter

75g (2½oz) full fat soft cheese

25g (1oz) icing sugar

20g (¾oz) desiccated coconut

'Tha Bodach na Nollaig a' tighinn a-nochd' is the Gaelic for 'Father Christmas is coming tonight'. These are easy to make with your kids to leave out on Christmas Eve for Santa.

METHOD

First, the brownie base. Heat the oven to 170°C fan (375°F). Line a 20cm x 30cm (8" x 12") baking tin with parchment. Gently melt the butter and the sugar together in a large pan. Once melted, take off the heat and add the chocolate. Stir until melted.

Beat in the eggs, then stir in the flour and the cocoa powder. Pour the brownie batter into the prepared tin and bake for 30 minutes, or until the top of the brownie is just firm.

Take out of the oven and leave to cool in the tin. Using a round cutter, cut a dozen circles from the brownie.

Lower the oven temperature to 100°C fan (250°F) for the meringue hats. Line a baking sheet with parchment. Beat the egg whites until they have doubled in size. Add the sugar, 1 tablespoon at a time along with the colouring paste (keep adding till you get the right colour), while you continue to whisk until they hold up in stiff peaks.

Fit a disposable piping bag with a round nozzle. Hold it vertically to the baking sheet and gently squeeze, pulling the bag up and away to make a peak. Make at least a dozen meringues.

Place in the oven for 1 hour, switch off the oven and leave the oven door slightly ajar for another 30 minutes.

Whip the butter and cream cheese together and sieve the icing sugar in a tablespoon at a time. Stir together until you get a thick frosting.

Place the brownie rounds on a board. Pipe the frosting on each brownie and scatter over a little coconut. Place a meringue hat on each, and a dot of frosting on top. Finally, roll up a wee bit of the leftover brownies into a ball and place it on the coconut frosting to make a nose.

Serve immediately to your family and Santa!

CHRISTMAS ROCKY ROAD

MAKES 24 SQUARES

INGREDIENTS

125g (4½oz) soft butter

300g (10½oz) dark chocolate

3 tablespoons golden syrup

200g (7oz) amaretti biscuits

50g (1¾oz) roughly chopped pistachios

30g (1oz) cranberries

100g (3½oz) mini marshmallows

½ orange, zested

Icing sugar, for dusting

This is Christmas Rocky Road with ALL the trimmings! Adding dark chocolate, amaretti biscuits, pistachios and cranberries gives them a more adult flavour – but I can't leave out the mini marshmallows. These no-bake treats are the perfect festive gift, if you can cope with letting them leave your house . . .

METHOD

Melt the butter, chocolate and golden syrup in a saucepan.

Break the amaretti biscuits into different sized chunks and add along with the pistachios, cranberries and marshmallows into the saucepan and stir everything together.

Tip into a 24cm (10") baking tin and press down, trying not to break the amaretti biscuits. Decorate with some extra chopped pistachios and orange zest before placing in the fridge for at least 2 hours.

Slice into blocks, dust with icing sugar and divide into gift bags for your friends and family.

FESTIVE HEBRIDEAN GIN

INGREDIENTS

1 orange, zested

1 lemon, zested

150g (5oz) mixed dried fruit
(you choose – sultanas,
raisins, currants)

5cm (2") piece of root ginger,
chopped

75g (2½oz) golden caster
sugar

2 vanilla pods, split

2 cinnamon sticks

1 teaspoon whole cloves

1 x 750ml bottle (or 3 cups)
Isle of Harris gin

Winter is made for infusions, capturing flavours to last through the colder months. This delicious homemade gin liqueur is brimming with festive flavours and will be ready to sip after just a few days. Serve as a warming aperitif or use it as the base for a Festive Fizz cocktail, topping it up with prosecco or champagne.

METHOD

Pare the zest of the orange and lemon with a vegetable peeler and add along with the dried fruit, ginger, sugar, vanilla pods, cinnamon sticks and cloves into a lidded jar. Pour in the gin and shake vigorously.

Leave to infuse in a cool, dark cupboard for 3 to 4 days, shaking every day. It should be a dark, golden colour when ready. Strain through a piece of muslin (I recommend you do this at least twice) and pour into sterilised bottles.

CHRISTMAS ICE CREAM

SERVES 6

INGREDIENTS

300ml (1¼ cups) double cream

500ml (2 cups) ready-made vanilla custard

50g (1¾oz) marzipan

400g (14oz) mincemeat

You can't beat a mince pie at Christmas, but I love finding new ways to use my homemade mincemeat. This is an easy-to-make, no-churn dessert which is like a festive version of rum and raisin ice cream. What's not to love?

You'll find my homemade mincemeat recipe in the first cookbook *Hebridean Baker: Recipes and Wee Stories from the Scottish Islands.*

METHOD

Gently whisk the cream in a bowl; try not to over-whisk. Blend the custard into the cream.

Roll small bites of marzipan into balls and stir through the cream and then fold in the mincemeat.

Spoon into a box suitable for the freezer and freeze for 1 hour. Take out of the freezer and stir the frozen and soft ice cream together. Repeat this two more times.

You can then keep in the freezer, bringing it out about 15 minutes before you serve. Serve in a bowl as you sit by the fire, or in waffle cones to your friends out in the snowy mountains!

CLEMENTINE UPSIDE-DOWN CAKE

YIELDS 8 SLICES

INGREDIENTS

For the clementine topping

3–4 clementines (depending on size)

4 tablespoons soft light brown sugar

60g (2oz) butter

For the cake

6 eggs, or 300g (10½oz)

300g (10½oz) self-raising flour

300g (10½oz) butter

300g (10½oz) sugar

1 teaspoon baking powder

1 teaspoon of vanilla essence

To finish

300ml (1¼ cups) double cream

4–5 tablespoons marmalade

Some cakes always receive an 'oooh', 'ahhh' or 'wow' from guests when I carry it to the dinner table, and my Clementine Upside-Down Cake is definitely one of them. Clementine is one of my favourite flavours of Christmas, but of course at other times of the year, you can use oranges instead.

The perfect way to make the cake is to weigh out your eggs once they are out of the shells. Then add exactly the same amount of sugar, self-raising flour and butter. The cakes should work perfectly every time. In the recipe I have estimated the weight of your eggs.

METHOD

Preheat the oven to 160°C fan (350°F). Butter and line two 20cm (8") cake tins with parchment paper

Start with the topping. Slice the clementines and pat dry on kitchen paper. Put the soft brown sugar and the butter in a saucepan and melt over a medium heat. Pour into one of the prepared cake tins and place the clementine slices snugly together on top of the syrup.

Put all the cake ingredients into a large mixing bowl and beat with a hand mixer for 1 minute, or until just combined. It's important not to beat the batter too much – just long enough to make it smooth.

As evenly as possible, spoon the mixture into each cake tin, covering the syrupy clementines in one tin.

Place both cake tins into the oven for 25 minutes or until a skewer comes out clean. Leave to rest in the tins for a few minutes before placing on a wire rack to cool (with the clementines facing upwards).

To decorate the cake, prepare the double cream by whipping it with an electric whisk until soft peaks form. Put the plain sponge on a plate and cover with a thick layer of marmalade. Then pipe or spread the whipped cream.

Place the clementine topped sponge on top and brush on a tablespoon of warmed marmalade. Finally, bring to the table and await the ohhhs, ahhhs and wows!

PANNETONE BREAD & BUTTER PUDDING

SERVES *4*

INGREDIENTS

5–7 slices of panettone

50g (1¾oz) softened butter

2 eggs

225ml (¾ cup +
    3 tablespoons) milk

150ml (½ cup +
    2 tablespoons) double
    cream

1 teaspoon vanilla extract

2 tablespoons caster sugar

Icing sugar, for dusting

This traditional Italian Christmas gift is the perfect replacement for white bread to make this a more festive pudding. This sweet bread filled with dried and candied fruit brings its warming flavours to this classic dish. There is no more comforting Christmas dessert than this!

METHOD

Preheat the oven to 140°C fan (325°F) and grease a 850ml (3½ cups) shallow baking dish with a wee bit of butter.

Slice and butter the panettone. Lay the slices in the dish in any order that makes you happy, but making sure you have crusts peeking out the top of the dish!

In a bowl, whisk together the eggs, milk and double cream, along with the vanilla and caster sugar.

Pour some of the creamy mixture over the slices of panettone and allow to rest for 5 minutes. Repeat the process, until all the mixture is used up.

Bake for 25 to 30 minutes until brown on top, but still a little wobbly.

Serve with a dusting of icing sugar and drowned in vanilla custard.

FIRST FOOTER MARTINI

MAKES 1

INGREDIENTS

300ml (1¼ cups) caster
sugar

150ml (½ cup +
2 tablespoons) water

40ml (2 tablespoons +
2 teaspoons) Jura Whisky

30ml (2 tablespoons) strong
espresso

15ml (1 tablespoon)
Frangelico

Dash of sugar syrup

3 coffee beans

Scotland's Hogmanay celebrations and traditions are famous around the
world. Welcoming a tall, dark, handsome man at your door after midnight
is definitely one of the highlights! First Footers traditionally will bring you a
piece of peat or coal to keep the fire going, a cake, usually a Black Bun
but most importantly a bottle of whisky! Here is a great cocktail to welcome
your First Footers to your home. *Bliadhna mhath ùr!*

METHOD

First, make the sugar syrup: dissolve the caster sugar in the water over a low
heat. Leave to cool and bottle for future use in cocktails. Store in the fridge.

Add whisky, espresso, Frangelico and sugar syrup to a cocktail shaker.
Shake very hard until foamy.

Strain into a martini glass and garnish with 3 coffee beans.

WHIPKÜL

SERVES 4

INGREDIENTS

100ml (⅓ cup +
   1 tablespoon) double
   cream

3 egg yolks

30g (1oz) caster sugar

2 tablespoons rum

Freshly grated nutmeg

This dish is traditionally served by the islanders of Shetland for breakfast on New Year's Day. What a way to start the year! Originally a Scandinavian recipe, this is a simple and luxurious festive treat. You can make it your own by adding layers of nuts, crushed biscuits or fruit compote (rhubarb would be perfect).

Whipkül is easy to prepare and best served immediately – marauding Vikings are optional!

METHOD

Whip the cream in a large bowl and set aside.

Bring a saucepan of water to a simmer, take off the heat and place a heatproof bowl on top without it touching the water.

Put the egg yolks, sugar and rum into the bowl and use an electric whisk for 7 or 8 minutes to mix together until very pale, thick and creamy.

Blend the egg mixture into the cream and fold together gently.

Spoon your Whipkül into glasses, dust with freshly grated nutmeg and serve immediately.

A BAKING PLAYLIST

MURT NA CEAPAICH
KIM CARNIE

•

A-NOCHD A' CHIAD OIDHCHE
'N FHOGHAIR
SIAN

•

ISLE OF EIGG
HÒ-RÒ

•

IAIN GHLINN CUAICH
EWEN HENDERSON

•

A' GHRIAN
**NITEWORKS FEAT.
KATHLEEN MACINNES**

•

DH'ÈIRICH MI MOCH
MADAINN CHEÒTHAR
JULIE FOWLIS

•

BÀGH SEANNABHAD
DUNCAN CHISHOLM

•

CIANALAS NA HEARACH
JENNA CUMMING

•

SHADOW TO THE LIGHT
(PIANO VERSION)
TIDE LINES

FEEL THE POWER
**GARY INNES FEAT.
MISCHA MACPHERSON**

•

SOLAS
VALTOS

•

ÒRAN AN AMADAIN BHÒIDHICH
HÒ-RÒ

•

YOU ARE MY HEART
ABIGAIL PRYDE

•

RIBINNEAN RÌOMHACH
JULIE FOWLIS

•

AIR AN TRAIGH
TRAIL WEST

•

TÈ BHEAG
BEINN LEE

•

SORAIDH LEIS A' BHREACAIN ÙR
**BRIAN Ò HEADHRA &
FIONNAG NICCHOINNICH
(FEAT ÒRLA NÌ EADHRA)**

•

GRÀDH GEAL MO CHRIDH'
ISBHEL MACASKILL

ACKNOWLEDGEMENTS

Thank you to . . .

Ali, Campbell and the team at Black & White Publishing for allowing me to continue the Hebridean Baker journey! Thanks to Clem and Thomas for all your help with the book. Ali, your support means the world to me.

Seonag, I couldn't have made this book without you. Thank you for being by my side in the kitchen.

Susie, the best photographer in the world!

My brothers Murdo and Colin, thank you for putting up with me!

Kyle and Oscar – keep chasing the cupcakes!

Margaret Ann at Harris Tweed Hebrides for dressing me and my bakes in the most beautiful tweeds.

Shona and Ria at Charles MacLeod Butchers – for your delicious recipe and keeping me stocked in black puddings!

Cathy and Jack at Braw Kilts and Ashley at House of Cheviot for the stunning kilts and socks.

Rhona, Paul, Karis, David and all the villagers of Cromore, taing mhòr.

Irene, Mairi, Shona, Mike, Iona and all the team at the Isle of Harris Distillery. Always making this Lewisman feel welcome across the border!

Donnie Morrison, Comunn Eachdraidh na Pairc, the Angus MacLeod Archive, Aunt Bellag, Aunt Louisa, Aunt Morag and Dolina MacLennan for great island stories.

Cathy Bhàn for inviting me to your kitchen and all the fun we had baking together!

Rachel at Jura Whisky, thanks for all the drams and wonderful support.

Kerri Anne Kelly at Caledonian MacBrayne for getting me over the Minch and back many times!

Taing mhòr do Mhàiri Anna airson a cuid comhairle leis a' Ghàidhlig.

Mairi, Julie and the Visit Outer Hebrides team, Historic Environment Scotland, Arnol Blackhouse and Marlene for all your help. Gearrannan Blackhouse Village. Coinneach Moireach and his tractor. Essence of Harris. Scott Bennett at Borvemor Cottages. Shona MacQueen for the Hebridean Baker slate and Sheena, the Harris Tweed Florist.

The duff man, Ùisdean – thanks for the inspiration! Joy for helping my Eurovision dreams come true!

Jeff and Dan for hiking over hills and peatbogs to help me get the best photographs.

Thanks Graham, Morven and the MacQueens for everything.

And finally, to the most loved pup in the Hebrides, Seòras.

ABOUT COINNEACH

Coinneach MacLeod was born and raised on the Isle of Lewis, the most northerly of the Outer Hebrides of Scotland. Inspired by traditional family recipes and homegrown produce, Coinneach rose to fame as the Hebridean Baker on TikTok in 2020. He has motivated his worldwide followers to bake, forage, learn Gaelic, enjoy a dram or two of whisky and to seek a more wholesome, simple life. Along with his partner Peter and their Westie pup Seòras, Coinneach's aim is to bring the best of the Scottish islands to a worldwide audience.

You can find Coinneach online at:

hebrideanbaker.com
@hebrideanbaker on TikTok
@hebridean_baker on Twitter
@hebrideanbaker on Instagram